NOVENAS
FOR THE CHURCH YEAR

NOVENAS
FOR THE CHURCH YEAR

Fr. Peter John Cameron, O.P.

Our Sunday Visitor Publishing Division
Our Sunday Visitor, Inc.
Huntington, Indiana 46750

Nihil Obstat
Msgr. Michael Heintz, Ph.D.
Censor Librorum

Imprimatur
✠ Kevin C. Rhoades
Bishop of Fort Wayne-South Bend
June 6, 2012

The *Nihil Obstat* and *Imprimatur* are official declarations that a
book is free from doctrinal or moral error. It is not implied that
those who have granted the *Nihil Obstat* and *Imprimatur* agree
with the contents, opinions, or statements expressed.

ISBN: 978-1-61278-540-0 (Inventory No. T1240)
eISBN: 978-1-61278-287-4
LCCN: 2012948711

Cover design: Lindsey Riesen / Interior Design: Dianne Nelson
Cover art: Shutterstock

PRINTED IN THE UNITED STATES OF AMERICA

For
Sister Marie Rita Syn of the Blessed Sacrament
Benedictines of the Congregation of Jesus Crucified
in honor of her
Golden Jubilee of Religious Profession

Serve the Lord with joy.
Amen! Alleluia!

TABLE OF CONTENTS

FOREWORD

"Numero deus impare gaudet."
(God rejoices in the odd number.)
— Virgil

THE CHURCH ENCOURAGES THE FAITHFUL to deepen their faith by taking advantage of all available means in harmony with the teachings of the Church. Especially venerable among these is the devotion known as the *novena*.

What Is a Novena?

The *Directory on Popular Piety and the Liturgy* says this about novenas:

> Throughout the middle ages many forms of popular piety gradually emerged or developed. Many of these have been handed down to our times: ... nucleuses of "sacred times" based on popular practices were constituted. These were often marginal to the rhythm of the liturgical year: sacred or profane fair days, tridua, octaves, novenas, months devoted to particular popular devotions.[1]

A novena is a prayer (or a series of prayers) said consecutively for nine days. The prayer — which can be either private or public — is recited daily as a preparation for a certain feast or in order to obtain some special favor.

The novena stands out as a spiritual exercise of hopeful yearning and expectation. It helps predispose the one who prays to receive the particular heavenly graces sought. At the same time, praying the same prayer nine days in a row builds up the confidence and gratitude of the believer through an experience of holy anticipation. As a prayer form, the novena incorporates two key qualities of efficacious prayer: trustful certainty and faith-filled perseverance.

St. Augustine points out that the deepest motive for prayer like the novena is the enlarging of desire:

> Our Lord and God does not want to know what we want (for he cannot fail to know it) but wants us rather to exercise our desire through our prayers, so that we may be able to receive what he is preparing to give us. His gift is very great indeed, but our capacity is too small and limited to receive it. That is why we are told: *Enlarge your desires.*[2]

The Nine of the Novena

According to a pious tradition, the concept of the novena finds its inspiration in the nine months during which the Christ-child was carried in the womb of his mother before Christmas. The Advent "O Antiphons" leading up to Christmas (December 17-23) have a novena-like quality about them (O Wisdom, O Adonai, O Root of Jesse, and so forth). The model and the first of all novenas was that prayerful awaiting undertaken by the apostles and the Blessed Virgin Mary in the Upper Room — the Cenacle — in the nine days between the Ascension of the Lord and Pentecost (see Acts 1:4, 13-14).

And yet our system of mathematics is "decimal": it is based on the number ten as the symbol of the entire method of numeration. Some suggest that since the number ten represents a kind of "perfect" number, the number nine — being just shy of ten —is the number of "imperfection." Praying from this position of nine's imperfection is deemed altogether fitting for fallen, mortal creatures like us. St. Jerome contends that, since "all the animals which Noah took into the ark by pairs were unclean," even numbers are iffy, and "odd numbers denote cleanness."[3]

An alternate view regards the number nine as the ideal. Martianus Capella, a pagan writer and developer of the system of the seven liberal arts of the fifth century, referred to the number nine as "the final part of harmony."[4] He declared that the number nine "is perfect, and is said to be more perfect because its form derives from the multiplication of the perfect triad." The Middle Ages saw an increase of interest in number symbolism and the spiritual significance of numbers, especially by several Cistercian numerologists.

A twelfth-century Spanish treatise on arithmetic known as *Queritur*, by an author called Johannes, highlights the prominence of the number nine. *Queritur* claims that the number nine (*nouenarius*) holds the position of leadership in all things and is the paradigm according to which the world was created — "the universe of things is contained within the nine." Johannes attributes to the number nine a "*plenitudo virtutum*" (fullness of virtue), since the number nine is the first number to contain a perfect number, a cubic number, and a plane number. The scholar Rabbi Abraham ibn Ezra (d. 1167) links Wisdom 11:20 — "*omnia mensura et numero et pondere disposuisti*" (You have arranged all things by measure and number and weight) —with the assertion that the number nine is the ordering principle of number.

Others allude to the fact that the New Testament lists nine fruits of the Holy Spirit (see Gal 5:22-23): love, joy, peace, patience, kindness, goodness, faithfulness, gentleness, and self-control. There are nine ranks of angels. Jesus died at the ninth hour (see Mt 27:46). The Bible identifies nine people who were stoned (see Lev 24:14; Num 15:36; Josh 7:25; Judg 9:53; 1 Kings 12:18; 21:10; 2 Chron 24:21; Acts 7:58-60; 14:19). St. Dominic prayed according to his famous nine ways of prayer. But this may be taking things too far.

How to Use This Book

For each of the feasts or special occasions treated in this book, you will find two things: a short reflection that treats the meaning of the feast or the occasion, and a novena prayer. Nine days in advance of the feast day or occasion you would like to commemorate, read the short reflection and then pray the novena prayer. On each of the following eight days, pray the novena prayer. After reciting the novena prayer, if you wish you may add an Our Father, a Hail Mary, and a Glory Be. You can do this either on your own or with others, for a total of nine consecutive days.

You need not be overly attached to the calendar to make beneficial use of this book. For example, when you feel inclined to pray in a special way for the pope, you might pray the novena prayer for the Chair of St. Peter (February 22). If you are concerned for someone who is out of work and looking for employment, or if you are dealing with problems at your job, consider praying the novena to St. Joseph the Worker (May 1). Anytime is an appropriate time to intercede for those who are ill by reciting the novena prayer for the World Day of the Sick (February 11). Or maybe you know a young person considering a religious vocation, or you want to give special prayerful support to those studying in the seminary. An ideal way would be to pray the novena prayer for the World Day of Prayer for Vocations (April).

(A special note about using this book: The Church's liturgical year contains a number of "moveable feasts" — feasts like Palm Sunday, Easter, Pentecost, and the First Sunday of Advent. Since these feasts do not have a set calendar date of their own, I have tried to place them in the month in which they frequently occur.)

A final hope is that the book's mini commentaries might provide fodder for priests and deacons in their preaching.

JANUARY

January 1

MARY, THE HOLY MOTHER OF GOD

THE SOURCE OF ALL OUR SORROW is what Adam did in Eden. How could he do such a thing? Maybe it was due to the fact that Adam was a man who never had a mother. So God decided to make sure that *that* never happened again. By God's grace, motherhood has become an indispensable element in the journey back to him.

How deep is the human need for a mother. In a book entitled *The Drama of the Gifted Child*, the psychiatrist Alice Miller explains how infants find themselves in the gaze of their mother. An infant needs to be mirrored by the mother. In fact, if the mother fails in this regard and instead projects her own fears and predicaments upon her baby, the child, failing to find himself in his mother's face, will seek that mirror for the rest of his life.[1] That is why God, in becoming incarnate, gives us a mother in whom we can find that total acceptance. The temptation to turn Christ into an abstraction or to reduce him to his message gets trounced by the Mother of God, who constantly makes Jesus flesh and blood for us again.

That is why Christ's parting command from the cross — "Behold, your mother!" (Jn 19:27) —

stands as the method for the whole of the Christian life. For a mother is not just the mother of our physical life but of our whole person. She possesses the unique ability to take our sorrows and turn them into joys, to imbue our life with the certainty of being loved that stays with us all throughout life. The Mother of God does all this and more.

No wonder Blessed John Paul II insists that not only does Mary lead us to Christ, but Christ leads us to his mother.[2] For the motherhood of Mary makes it possible for us to have intimacy with God. Whenever the Mother of God loves us, she gives us Jesus. As Blessed Guerric of Igny (d. 1157) says, "Mary is the Mother of all who are born again to new life. She is the Mother of him who is the Life by which all things live."[3]

NOVENA PRAYER

O Blessed Virgin Mary, from the cross your Son appointed you to be Mother of the entire human race. This great gift of Jesus reveals how much I need you to be my Mother. O Mother of God, deepen my love for you. You lead us to your Son, and your Son leads us back to you. May I find in your maternal love the total acceptance I need from moment to moment to live my life.

Mother of the Life, by which all things live, be the Mother of my whole person. Take my sorrows and turn them into joys. Mold me in your way of holiness. Whenever you love us, you give us Jesus. Bless me with the certainty of being loved, and help me to grow in intimacy with God. With confidence in your maternal mediation, I entrust to you these my intentions: (mention your request here).

January 1

WORLD DAY OF PEACE

SINCE 1967, the Vatican has designated January 1 as World Day of Peace. According to the *Directory on Popular Piety and the Liturgy*,

> This day is reserved "for intense prayer for peace, education towards peace and those values inextricably linked with it, such as liberty, fraternal solidarity, the dignity of the human person, respect for nature, the right to work, the sacredness of human life, and the denunciation of injustices which trouble the conscience of man and threaten peace."[4]

From the moment Jesus begins to preach, he proclaims: "Blessed are the peacemakers" (Mt 5:9). Peace is the answer to the primordial longings that make up the desire for happiness in us. Paradoxically, peace usually begins at the point where it seems most unlikely: with the recognition of our sinfulness — the cause of our conflicts and evil.[5] True peace cannot be conceived "merely [as] the absence of war"; neither is it simply the balance of power maintained between adversaries (see *Catechism of the Catholic Church* [CCC] 2304). St. Peter Chrysologus (d. 450) speaks of peace as the plenitude that fulfills all desires.[6]

What, then, is the peace we are praying for on this day? "He who, on the cross, suffered and overcame the lies and the hatred of mankind was peace itself…. In giving his peace he did not simply give something — he gave himself. The Lord gives himself to his own as peace."[7] In order to be true peacemakers, Pope Benedict XVI says,

We must educate ourselves in compassion, solidarity, working together, fraternity, in being active within the community and concerned to raise awareness about national and international issues and the importance of seeking adequate mechanisms for the redistribution of wealth, the promotion of growth, cooperation for development and conflict resolution.[8]

We work for peace with complete certainty because Jesus Christ himself promises it to us as a gift of his resurrection: "Peace I leave with you; my peace I give to you; not as the world gives do I give to you" (Jn 14:27). Peacemakers make Jesus present in the world. "The power of peace … overcomes nothingness and death" (Pope Benedict XVI).[9]

Novena Prayer

Loving Father, with great confidence we pray that the peace of heaven will reign on earth. For at your Son's resurrection, Jesus promised to give us the peace that the world cannot give. We cannot live without peace. Bless every nation with divine peace. Heal all injustice, division, discord, hatred, and violence. Put an end to wars, persecution, civil strife, discrimination, terrorism, and oppression. Save us from the enemies to peace: egoism, dissension, discouragement, selfishness, and doubt.

Gospel peace is serenity of thought, tranquillity of mind, simplicity of heart, the bond of love, and the fellowship of charity. It calms us and disposes us to partake of eternal things. May the peace of Christ radiate through us, inclining us to spread that peace to others. Permit me to be a true peacemaker in the world. United to the intercession of Mary, Queen of Peace, I offer my intentions: (mention your request here).

January 3

THE MOST HOLY NAME OF JESUS

THE HIGH POINT of the angelic announcements to both Mary and Joseph is the revelation of the name they will give their child: Jesus. The bestowal of the Holy Name imbues Mary and Joseph with the supernatural courage and resolve needed to accept their God-given destiny. The gift of a name is a privileged honor: a gesture of trust and intimacy, of handing oneself over to another to be known — for a name is something sacred, an icon of the person who bears it.

But unlike other names, as the *Catechism* teaches, the name of Jesus "contains the presence it signifies," which means it "contains all" (CCC 2666). Blind Bartimaeus understands this. Upon hearing that Christ is passing by, he cries out, "Jesus, Son of David, have mercy on me!" (Mk 10:47). And the Good Thief on the cross makes bold to beg, "Jesus, remember me when you come into your kingly power" (Lk 23:42). As the repentant apostle Peter will proclaim, "There is no other name under heaven given among men by which we must be saved" (Acts 4:12). God reveals and gives us his name in order to restore in us the image of God lost at the Fall.

Jesus wants us to have and to use his name — "the highest honor of the believer" (St. Bernardine of Siena).[10] The night before he dies, our Savior asks us repeatedly to pray in his name for all that we need (see Jn 14:13, 14; 15:16; 16:23, 24, 26). Christ promises that when two or three of us gather in his name, he is there in our midst (see Mt 18:20). When we dare to believe in the name of Jesus, he gives us "power to become children of God" (Jn 1:12). We have "life in his name" (Jn 20:31), for "you were washed, you were sanctified, you were justified in the name of the Lord Jesus Christ" (1 Cor 6:11).

Prayerful recalling of the name of Jesus, says the fourteenth-century mystic Richard Rolle, purges our sin, kindles our heart, clarifies our soul, removes anger, wounds in love, chases the devil, puts out dread, and opens heaven.[11]

NOVENA PRAYER

Lord Jesus, thank you for the precious gift of your Holy Name, by which you draw close to us, you free us from our sins, you offer us your friendship, and you love us with the tenderness of your heart. Jesus, you promised on the night before you died that anything we ask for in your Name you will do. When your apostle Peter invoked your Holy Name, the lame beggar at the Beautiful Gate was healed and began to walk. Everyone who calls on the Holy Name of Jesus will be saved.

I believe in your Holy Name and hope in the eternal life it promises. Let your Holy Name be my strength and sustenance. May this highest honor of the believer always be in my heart and on my lips. United with you in the power of your Holy Name, I entrust my intentions: (mention your request here).

January 6

THE EPIPHANY OF THE LORD

BY THE INCARNATION, the Son of God in a certain way unites himself with every human being. The Epiphany manifests this union to the world. Pope Benedict XVI says it was as though the Magi "had always been waiting for [the Epiphany] star."[12] What prompts them to leave every-thing is a deep desire. To follow the mystery, we must risk coming out of ourselves and moving beyond our way of perceiving things. The Magi prostrate themselves before the newborn child, for "no one … can approach God here [on earth] except by kneeling before the manger and ador ing him" in the hidden weakness of his infancy (CCC 563).

The Magi, says St. Edith Stein (d. 1942), repre-sent seekers from all lands who live with a pure longing for truth that goes beyond boundaries. All of the treasures of the world are like dust com-pared with the Incarnate Truth in Mary's arms.[13] This sums up the whole law of human existence: bowing down before what is infinitely great (Fy-odor Dostoevsky).[14]

St. Leo the Great (d. 461) tells us that the only way God can be worthily honored is by present-ing him with what he has already given us.[15] The gifts the Magi offer represent their God-given desires. The gold fit for royalty begs, "You, Jesus, come and be my king. Don't allow me to be ruled by my thoughts, my feelings, my understanding." The gift of incense confesses Christ's divinity and our need to worship him with the worship that saves us from disintegration. And the myrrh rev-erences Christ's sacred humanity destined to end in death on the cross — a death that is our glory to share.

The Magi return to their country by another way: that of faith, hope, and especially charity. In Charles Dickens' *A Christmas Carol*, the ghost of Jacob Marley cries, "Why did I walk through crowds of fellow beings with my eyes turned down, and never raise them to that blessed Star which led the Wise Men to a poor abode? Were there no poor homes to which its light would have conducted *me*?"[16] That is where the Magi are headed now.

NOVENA PRAYER

Loving God, in every time and place you come close to us. You never cease to draw us to yourself. Our desire for you is written in our heart. Thank you for the ways that you break into my world and attract me to yourself. You call me to seek you, to know you, and to love you with all my heart. Give me the courage to leave behind old ways of thinking and acting, and to follow where you lead me — for communion with you is our truest dignity.

Make my life one of unceasing worship and adoration. Let me always embrace the Truth I find in the arms of the Blessed Virgin Mary: Jesus Christ our Savior. May the witness of my life of faith manifest your goodness to the world. United to the Light revealed to the nations, I offer you my intentions: (mention your request here).

January

THE BAPTISM OF THE LORD

A PUZZLING QUESTION raised by the mystery of the Baptism of the Lord is this: Why would someone sinless ever present himself to be baptized? The Lord soon will tell us that he has come to call sinners (see Lk 5:32), and he begins to issue that call by coming into our midst in the semblance of a sinner. Consider: If we were to discover ourselves among the immense throng pressing that day toward John the Baptist for baptism and suddenly spotted Jesus in our midst, we would conclude that he was "one of us." And that first impression would be a consolation which Christ intends in his act of coming forward to be baptized. For Jesus knows full well that one of the most devastating effects of sin is the way it imposes upon us the terrible loneliness of life. Into that sin and its attendant loneliness steps Jesus, consenting to be numbered among sinners (see CCC 536).

This is a gesture of self-emptying: Jesus at the Jordan voluntarily submits himself to the baptism "intended for sinners, in order to 'fulfill all righteousness' (Mt 3:15)" — that is, to do his Father's will (CCC 1224). Through his baptism, the Lord accepts and begins his mission as " 'the Lamb of God, who takes away the sin of the world' (Jn 1:29)" (CCC 536, cf. Is 53:12). The baptism with water anticipates Jesus' Calvary baptism of blood. As well as anticipating his death, Jesus' baptism prefigures and proclaims our own baptism. Up to this moment, Jesus has been living a "hidden life" at home. What draws Jesus out of his hiddenness is our acknowledgment of our sin. Christ continues to come to us personally, as he did that day at the Jordan River, when we confess ourselves to be sinners.

Following the example set for us by Jesus the Beggar, we come before God the Father acknowledging him with our nothingness. The baptism of Jesus changes everything, making us new creatures. From this moment on, whenever people face their sins, they no longer do so alone. As we look at our sins, we see that there is Someone filled with the Father's love, looking at us with tender, untellable mercy.

Novena Prayer

Loving Father, the baptism of Jesus reveals that you want each one of us to approach you in our nothingness, confident in your mercy. At the Jordan River you spoke from the heavens, "This is my beloved Son, with whom I am well pleased" (Mt 3:17). Your voice is meant for us as well. Let me never be afraid or hesitant to come before you confessing my sins. Let my whole life be a begging for your mercy.

Through Baptism, you claim me for yourself, and unite me with all Christians. Help me to live out my baptismal promises fully. Allow me to grow in goodness through the moral virtues. May my baptism bear fruit in the witness of a holy life, abounding in charity, especially toward those most in need. United with my humble Redeemer who offered himself to you in baptism, I offer you my intentions: (mention your request here).

January

Week of Prayer for Christian Unity

The night before he died, Jesus prayed to the Father on behalf of his disciples: "… that they may all be one" (Jn 17:21). Each year from January 18 to 25, this heartfelt desire of our Lord is renewed in the Church's observance of the Week of Prayer for Christian Unity. This week, as the *Directory on Popular Piety and the Liturgy* points out, affords Catholics, with Christians from other ecclesial communities, "a special occasion for common prayer for the grace of Christian unity, to offer to God their common anxieties, to give thanks to God, and to implore his assistance."[17] The *Catechism* teaches that

> Christ always gives his Church the gift of unity, but the Church must always pray and work to maintain, reinforce, and perfect the unity that Christ wills for her.... The desire to recover the unity of all Christians is a gift of Christ and a call of the Holy Spirit. (CCC 820, cf. *UR* 1)

This is why in the Solemn Intercessions on Good Friday the Church directs us: "Let us pray also for all our brothers and sisters who believe in Christ, / that our God and Lord may be pleased / ... to gather them together and keep them in his one Church." Even more, the Roman Missal provides *three* Masses for the Unity of Christians. In those Masses, we pray to God that "those whom one Baptism has consecrated / may be joined together by integrity of faith / … in the bond of charity," and "that the hearts of believers / may be united in your praise and in repentance together."[18] For we must never forget that "the gathering together of the Church is, as it were, God's reaction to the chaos provoked by sin" (CCC 761).

Pope Benedict XVI stresses that through Jesus' prayer for unity, the truth of his mission becomes visible to the world, for God brings about a unity inexplicable on the basis of humankind's efforts. God's unity "overcomes the world's inherent tendency toward fragmentation." It remains "a unity that can come into existence only from God … and yet is so concrete in its appearance that in it we are able to see God's power at work."[19]

Novena Prayer

Loving Father, the greatest possible joy is unity — the unity you share with the Son and the Holy Spirit in the communion of the Blessed Trinity. In the days after Easter, the proof of Christ's resurrection was the visible unity of the Church. What united so many disparate people was the presence of Jesus Christ alive in their midst. Everything in us craves this unity. Bless us with the Presence of Jesus so that the unity which your Son desired may become a living reality.

Please allow all that unites Christians to prevail over whatever separates them. Give us the grace to maintain, reinforce, and perfect the unity that Christ wills for his Church. Especially convert me from anything that inhibits me from contributing to true Christian unity. United with your beloved Son, who prayed that all may be one, I offer you my intentions: (mention your request here).

January 22

DAY OF PENANCE FOR VIOLATIONS TO THE DIGNITY OF THE HUMAN PERSON

IN ALL THE DIOCESES of the United States of America, January 22 — the anniversary of the Supreme Court decision *Roe vs. Wade* (1973) legalizing abortion — is observed as a particular day of penance for violations to the dignity of the human person committed through acts of abortion. It is a day of prayer for the full restoration of the legal protection of unborn children and the legal guarantee of the right to life (see *General Instruction on the Roman Missal*, 373).

The law of nature demands that a human being be recognized as having the rights of a person from the very first moment of that human being's existence. The chief of these rights "is the inviolable right of every innocent" human conceived in his or her mother's womb to life (CCC 2270). For this reason, the Church remains unflinching in teaching that human life must be respected and protected absolutely from the moment of conception.

And the Church acts heroically to carry out this conviction. While this day stands as one of profound mourning for the death of countless millions of unborn children, it at the same time seeks the transformation of all of society. For "when a society moves towards the denial or suppression of life, it ends up no longer finding the necessary motivation and energy to strive for man's true good."[20]

Accordingly, Blessed John Paul II (d. 2005) teaches that

> We need to bring the Gospel of Life to the heart of every man and woman, and to make it penetrate every part of society…. It is the proclamation of a living God who is close to us, who calls us to profound communion with himself and awakens in us the certain hope of eternal life…. It is the presentation of human life as a life of

relationship, a gift of God, the fruit and
sign of his love.[21]

Every human life is a gift from God. The Lord
declares, "I have set before you life and death,
blessing and curse; therefore choose life" (Dt
30:19).

NOVENA PRAYER

*Loving Father, the Church firmly believes that hu-
man life, even if weak and suffering, is always a
splendid gift of God's goodness. The Church stands
for life, even in the face of the pessimism and selfishness that cast a shadow over the world. Strengthen
those who devote their lives to defending the human person from all who plot against and harm
life. Be with all witnesses to the Culture of Life.
Bless the Church with clear and stronger conviction to promote human life by every means and
to defend it against all attacks. Protect the most
defenseless of your people. Raise up civil servants
who will enact just laws and protect the rights and
freedom of all.*

*Especially endow me with the courage and con-
viction to proclaim the Gospel of Life in every circumstance. United with Jesus, the Lord of Life, I offer
you my intentions: (mention your request here).*

January 25

THE CONVERSION OF ST. PAUL

BLESSED JOHN HENRY NEWMAN (d. 1890) looked upon conversion as nothing more than a deeper discovery of what we already truly desire. Conversion happens at the level of desire. It is the restoration of what makes us truly human.

Saul of Tarsus, the "Pharisee, a son of Pharisees" (Acts 23:6), had often prayed in the Psalms, "You have said, 'Seek my face.' My heart says to you, 'Your face, LORD, do I seek.' ... Bow your heavens, O LORD, and come down! ... Flash forth the lightning.... Stretch forth your hand from on high, rescue me and deliver me" (Ps 27:8-9; 144:5, 6, 7). And that is *exactly* what happened when Saul encountered Christ on the road to Damascus:

> Suddenly a light from heaven flashed about him.... [He] heard a voice saying to him, "Saul, Saul, why do you persecute me? ... I am Jesus...." ... They led [Saul] by the hand. (Acts 9:3, 4, 5, 8)

Pope Benedict XVI speaks of conversion as an act of obedience toward a reality that does not originate from us, that precedes us: the concrete God.[22] Similarly, for Blessed Pope John Paul II, conversion means returning to God "through evaluating earthly realities in the unfailing light of his truth."[23] The proof of Paul's conversion is his profession, "For to me to live is Christ" (Phil 1:21). Conversion is a conversion to the will and design of God: "It is no longer I who live, but Christ who lives in me" (Gal 2:20). "Conversion to Christ," says Pope Benedict, "ultimately means this: to exit the illusion of self-sufficiency in order to discover and accept one's own need — the need of others and God, the need of His forgiveness and His friendship."[24]

Various daily acts cause our conversion to grow: examining our conscience and admitting our faults; undertaking works of penance and reconciliation; receiving the correction others give us; reaching out to the poor; standing up for what is right and just; accepting the suffering and persecution that come our way; desiring to better our life (see CCC 1435). The key to conversion? Keeping our focus on the cross of Jesus Christ, for "the human heart is converted by looking upon [the Crucified] whom our sins have pierced" (CCC 1432, cf. Jn 19:37; Zech 12:10).

Novena Prayer

Glorious St. Paul, your conversion is a powerful witness to the world that God loves us and does not give up on us, no matter how far we stray. Help me to live a life of ongoing conversion. True conversion means converting my life to the design of God — the plan he has for me right now. Pray that I will love God's will and providence for me. May every circumstance of my life be an occasion to change my way of thinking, to renounce self-will, and to surrender myself to the wisdom and tenderness of Jesus Christ, who is acting to make me his saint.

May faith move me to believe that God can and will change the things in me that seem impossible. May the witness of my life inspire other sinners to conversion. In this confidence, I entrust to you these, my intentions: (mention your request here).

FEBRUARY

February 2

THE PRESENTATION OF THE LORD

THE PRESENTATION OF THE LORD is celebrated forty days after Christmas. The feast commemorates that day when the child Jesus is presented in the Temple by his parents, Mary and Joseph: a sacred encounter in which the Incarnate Savior comes mystically to meet his believing people. For this reason, from the early centuries of the Church, this mystery was called the "Feast of the Meeting." It is also named "Candlemas," for on this day candles are blessed, and the faithful process with them, singing, "A light for revelation to the Gentiles."

Jesus regarded the Temple as the dwelling of his Father, and thus the unique, "privileged place of encounter with God" (CCC 584). The Presentation of the Lord reveals Jesus to be the Son who belongs to the Father (see CCC 529). As we witness this blessed exchange, we long to be caught up in this sacred encounter — to become part of this belonging. In fact, the bearing of the baby Jesus to this sacred dwelling has a Eucharistic dimension: Mary comes to offer the very self of her Son to the Father, just as Jesus himself ultimately will do at the Last Supper.

We unite ourselves with the humanity of the infant Christ, for Jesus models for us an indispensable truth we are prone to forget: "Man … cannot fully find himself except through a sincere gift of himself."[1] Our life is meant to be a neverending presentation of our self to the Father — a constant faith-filled handing over of our lives to God in a gift of self. By that sacrifice we hope that God will be in our hearts even as he is in his holy Temple; we beg for just that when we pray, "Our Father who art in heaven" (see CCC 2794).

That angry day in the future when Christ will be incited to cleanse the Temple will tragically come about because people disregard the desire for today's encounter. Jesus will woo us back to that encounter by identifying "*himself* with the Temple [and thereby] presenting himself as God's definitive dwelling-place among [people]" (CCC 586, cf. Jn 2:21; Mt 12:6; emphasis mine).

NOVENA PRAYER

Loving Father, at the Presentation in the Temple Mary and Joseph offered the infant Jesus to you in consecration. That act reveals Jesus to be the Son who belongs to you. Let me be part of that belonging. Simeon's life was one of expectant waiting for the arrival of your Son. Make my life one of con-

stant attentiveness to the Presence of Jesus Christ. Fill me with Anna's patience and piousness.

As your Son was presented in the Temple, so may I present myself to you in purity of mind and heart. May the grace of this mystery enable me to live each moment as a gift of self. United with the Blessed Virgin Mary, I will not fear the swords that may pierce my heart. Rather, united with your Son, the light of revelation who has come into the world, I offer you my intentions: (mention your request here).

February 11

OUR LADY OF LOURDES/ WORLD DAY OF THE SICK

BLESSED JOHN PAUL II established the commemoration of Our Lady of Lourdes to be the annual World Day of the Sick. In his message for the first observance of the day in 1993, the pope spoke of it as "a special occasion for growth, with an attitude of *listening, reflection,* and *effective commitment* in the face of the great mystery of pain and illness…. A special time … of offering one's suffering for the good of the Church and of reminding everyone to see in his sick brother or sister the face of Christ."[2]

Such confidence flows from the apparitions of Our Lady to St. Bernadette Soubirous (d. 1879) and from the thousands of subsequent healings at the miraculous grotto in Lourdes. Pope Benedict XVI assures us that we are healed not by sidestepping or fleeing from suffering but "by our capacity for accepting it, maturing through it, and finding meaning through union with Christ, who suffered with infinite love."[3] Léon Bloy (d. 1917) intuited this in his now famous observation: "There are places in the heart that do not yet exist; suffering has to enter in for them to come to be."[4] Sickness opens our hearts to a divine truth: "Christ did not come to remove suffering, or to explain it away, but to fill it with his presence" (Paul Claudel).[5] Sickness is one way of "carrying in the body the death of Jesus, so that the life of Jesus may also be manifested in our bodies" (2 Cor 4:10).

Pope John Paul II assures us that "in suffering there is concealed a particular *power that draws a person interiorly close to Christ*…. It is suffering, more than anything else, which clears the way for the grace which transforms human souls. Suffering, more than anything else, makes present … the powers of the Redemption."[6]

We join Pope Leo XIII (d. 1903) in praying to Our Lady of Lourdes, "May the Virgin Mother, who once cooperated through her love with the birth of the faithful into the Church, now be the means and guardian of our salvation; may she return the tranquillity of peace to troubled souls; may she hasten the return of Jesus Christ in private and public life."[7]

NOVENA PRAYER

Our Lady of Lourdes, your miraculous presence in the grotto of Massabielle has inspired countless souls to look with hope beyond their infirmity and affliction to you. It is in times of pain that the ultimate questions about the meaning of life make themselves acutely felt. And at those moments you are always close! On this World Day of the Sick, show special solicitude to the sick and the suffering, especially those who are dear to me. Blessed Virgin, help me to offer my own suffering for the good of the Church and for the relief of those consumed by illness.

Immaculate Mother, return the tranquillity of peace to all troubled souls, especially to those who are alone and despairing. Increase my capacity to be compassionate and generous to the sick. Intercede for their healing. United in your immaculate love, I confide to you my intentions: (mention your request here).

February

ASH WEDNESDAY

TODAY WE ENTER into Lent's forty days of holy penitence. The *Directory on Popular Piety and the Liturgy* states that "the act of putting on ashes symbolizes fragility and mortality, and the need to be redeemed by the mercy of God" as well as an "attitude of internal penance ... clearly conscious of the need to turn the mind towards those realities which really count."[8] St. Basil the Great (d. 379) observes that the life of the human being reaches fulfillment through the succession of many deaths.[9]

This is why it is customary during Lent to practice mortification. Keep in mind: *God* does not need the self-imposed suffering we undergo, but *we* need to become detached from the things we would want outside of God. The purpose of our spiritual suffering is to unmask the lies we try to live by and to open our soul to the Father so that, together with Jesus, we may receive everything from him.

"The root of sin," says Pope Benedict XVI, "lies in the refusal to hear the Word of the Lord, and to accept in Jesus ... the forgiveness which opens us to salvation."[10] Sin turns us inward, makes us live on the surface of ourselves, and separates us from others. Through the holy detachment effected by mortification we become absorbed in what God wants for us. With great wisdom, Father Raniero Cantalamessa notes that the basic sin of egoism cannot be removed through the observance of law but only through a re-establishing of the friendship with God that Adam and Eve lost in Eden.[11] Lent is the invitation to re-establish that friendship. Thus, the most perfect mortification is *an act of love to God* that takes us out of ourselves, transporting us into the love of the Beloved.

When we love, our energy is not caught up in our thoughts that keep us closed in on ourselves. Rather, love directs all our energy to the *person* we love. "Every penance that increases love is good; any penance that narrows and preoccupies the soul is harmful" (Hans Urs von Balthasar).[12] Let our Lenten acts of love be unceasing!

NOVENA PRAYER

Loving Father, may I live this Lent as an unceasing act of love for you. Let me grow in understanding of the riches hidden in Christ. In my prayer, grant me a spirit to see what must be done and the strength to do what is right. Make me radiant in your presence with the strength of my yearning for you. By my fasting, fortify my resolve to carry out your loving commands. Bless me with an increase in devoutness of life so that I may be found steadfast in faith. And by my almsgiving, renew and purify my heart so that I may hold to the things that eternally endure.

May my self-denial of those things that are superfluous be translated into good works and solidarity with the poor. United with your Son, who makes his way to Calvary, I offer you my intentions: (mention your request here).

February 22

THE CHAIR OF ST. PETER

JESUS DECLARES TO HIS APOSTLE: "You are Peter, and on this rock I will build my Church.... I will give you the keys of the kingdom of heaven, and whatever you bind on earth shall be bound in heaven, and whatever you loose on earth shall be loosed in heaven" (Mt 16:18, 19). That God-given jurisdiction entrusted to Simon Peter is symbolized in the Chair of St. Peter (when a pope speaks *ex cathedra* — that is, "from the chair" — he gives an infallible teaching).

The feast of the Chair of St. Peter celebrates the fact that Christ appointed the apostle Peter to be the first of all the apostles and the visible head of the whole Church. At the same time, the Chair represents the teaching authority — the Magisterium — of the successors of Peter. The task of the Magisterium is the same as that of a good shepherd: to keep safe the People of God, preventing them from wandering off in mistaken or misleading ideas, and guiding them so that they can profess and practice the Catholic faith in full freedom and truth (see CCC 890). The Holy See wields the authority to govern the Church, "to absolve sins, to pronounce doctrinal judgments, and to make disciplinary decisions in the Church" through the Petrine office (CCC 553).

We must not forget, though, that in a certain sense the first "chair of Peter" was the seat he took by the fire when he denied knowing Jesus Christ (see Mt 26:69-75). Yet despite the scandalous enormity of his sin, Peter (unlike Judas) did not capitulate to despair. From the depths of the fisherman's tears of repentance, Christ elevates Peter to be *caput*, Head of the Church, Vicar of Christ. Seated once again by a fire, Peter hears the risen Jesus ask him, "Do you love me?" When Peter utters his famous threefold profession of love, Christ confers upon him his mission as Chief Shepherd:

"Feed my sheep" (Jn 21:15-18). Pope Benedict XVI says that since the Chair represents the pope's mission as the guide of the entire People of God, celebrating the Chair of Peter "means attributing a strong spiritual significance to it and recognizing it as a privileged sign of the love of God, the eternal Good Shepherd, who wanted to gather his whole Church and lead her on the path of salvation."[13]

Novena Prayer

Loving Father, in the tender mercy of your Son, we are not like sheep without a shepherd. You have blessed us with a Good Shepherd in the successor of St. Peter, our Holy Father. Deepen my reverence for the pope and for the Petrine office. Through the grace of the Chair of St. Peter, you shield the Church from error and preserve her from what is harmful. May I be always grateful for the authority the Holy Father exercises in the name of Jesus Christ, for you know how much we need in our lives an authority who will open our hearts continually.

Bless, protect, and strengthen our pope so that he will carry out his apostolic mission in the way that glorifies you. Increase my knowledge of the teachings of the Church and deepen my obedience. United in your beloved Son, I offer these intentions: (mention your request here).

February

World Marriage Day

THE CHURCH OBSERVES World Marriage Day the second Sunday in February. The Lord, desiring to make visible the depths of his love, raised marriage to the dignity of a sacrament. A husband and a wife consent to give themselves to each other "mutually and definitively" in "a covenant of faithful and fruitful love" (CCC 1662).

The indissoluble unity of a man and a woman joined in the sacrament of Matrimony symbolizes the definitive and irrevocable love offered to us by the Bridegroom, Jesus Christ. The perpetual and exclusive marital bond that arises between spouses represents God's absolute and unfailing love toward his people. St. Paul urges Christian husbands to "love your wives, as Christ loved the Church and gave himself up for her," for "this is a great mystery … in reference to Christ and the Church."

The grace proper to the sacrament of Matrimony is ordered to perfecting the couple's love, to strengthening their unbreakable union, to the procreation and education of children, and to helping each other achieve sanctity. Christ dwells with the Christian spouses, healing the wounds of sin in them. He gives them the power to take up their crosses and follow him, to forgive each other, to overcome self-absorption, and to bear each other's burdens. In loving each other with the love with which Christ loves the Church, the spouses open themselves to each other; "to mutual aid and to self-giving"; to "supernatural, tender, and fruitful love"; and to a communion of one flesh "confirmed, purified, and completed by communion in Jesus Christ" (CCC 1609, 1642, 1644).

The joyful fidelity and the fertility of Christian spouses witness to the truth of God's faithful love; marriage becomes "an efficacious sign of Christ's presence" (CCC 1613). The Redeemer comes to restore the original order of creation disturbed by sin, and the sacrament of Matrimony is at the heart of that re-creation: "God's creation is good; his forgiveness restores its joy; marriage is a sacrament because it, in its unique way, makes this known. In this way, it is a source of grace, first for those who share in it, then for others."[14]

NOVENA PRAYER

Loving God, you yourself are the author of Matrimony. Jesus our Savior enters the lives of married Christians through the sacrament of Matrimony, as God of old made himself present through a cove-

nant of love and fidelity. The purposes and benefits with which you have endowed the sacred bond of marriage bear on the dignity, stability, and prosperity of the human race, the family itself, and the whole of human society.

Just as Jesus loved the Church and handed himself over on her behalf, may spouses love each other with perpetual fidelity through mutual self-giving. Protect the sanctity of marriage. Strengthen the love between married couples. Keep them faithful. Make them holy parents. Heal and reunite separated spouses, and be close to those experiencing difficulties in their marriage. Bless newlyweds and those preparing for their wedding. United in Jesus the Bridegroom, I offer you these intentions: (mention your request here).

MARCH

March 19

St. Joseph, Spouse of the Blessed Virgin Mary

To St. Joseph, God entrusted his most valuable treasures and the beginning of our redemption. This feast commemorates the glories of St. Joseph, recalling especially his spousal relationship with the Blessed Virgin Mary. For, as Blessed John Paul II tells us, Joseph's "singular dignity and his rights regarding Jesus" derive "from his marriage to Mary."[1] In this, we honor St. Joseph's heroic faith, hope, and love.

The depth of Joseph's love as husband appears when he discovers his betrothed to be with child. Divine Mercy that had come to take flesh had already taken hold of Joseph's heart. This is why Joseph the "just man" did not expose Mary to the law. Condemned as an adulteress, Mary would have been subject to the crime's sentence: death by stoning (or, earlier in history, by burning). Before the execution, she would have been stripped naked, her hair cropped.

As for his faith, Joseph was so sensitively predisposed to the divine will in all its subtlety that he acceded to God even in his sleep. All the angel announced in the dream — *Son of David ... have*

*no fear … Holy Spirit … Jesus … will save his people
from their sins … the virgin shall be with child …
Emmanuel* — corresponded with the expectations
of Joseph's rectified heart (see Mt 1:20-23). In un-
conditional obedience, Joseph took Mary into his
home as his wife. By this act of faith, God's inscru-
table providence secures an ingenious way of being preserved, for tradition holds that Mary's marriage to Joseph became the means of hiding three
mysteries from the devil: the virginity of Mary, the
virginal birth of the Son of God, and the identity of
God's Son as he died on the cross.

Joseph's hope shows in the total absence of
any indignation or resentment regarding the
"modification" made to his marriage. As Pope
John Paul II explains, Joseph found in the Holy
Spirit the very source of the conjugal love that
he experienced as a man — a love which proved
to be greater than any natural love Joseph could
ever have expected within the limits of his human heart.[2] Ultimately, "God … gave Joseph to
Mary in order that *he might share*, through the
marriage pact, in her own sublime greatness."[3]

Novena Prayer

*Glorious St. Joseph, you came to share in the sub-
lime greatness of God's Mother by taking Mary to*

be your wife. Pray that I may partake of your faith by which you accepted divine providence, promptly obeying the will of God. Through your venerable silence, may I grow in a spirit of recollection. You gave God's Son his name; help me always to call on the Holy Name of Jesus in trust. Enable me to love the Blessed Virgin Mary as you do. May my love for Mary take precedence over all my plans, preconceptions, and self-reliance.

Bless me with your hope when circumstances become overwhelming or my problems seem impossible. Let me do what you do: look at the face of Mary, icon of the Father's love. To you, who protected the Mother of God and her Son from deadly danger, I offer my intentions: (make your request here).

March 25

THE ANNUNCIATION OF THE LORD

A PAINTING ENTITLED *The Annunciation* by the Venetian artist Tintoretto (d. 1594) shows a house in cutaway. On one side of the exposed wall sits the Blessed Virgin Mary prayerfully receiving the annunciation of the archangel. On the other side, we see the world lying in ruination: rubble, havoc, chaos, and utter devastation. The world without Jesus Christ is one of unspeakable misery. But when Mary speaks her *fiat*, her "yes" to the Holy Spirit, the never-ending Newness who is Jesus Christ changes everything.

Even after the Fall, something positive and urgent drives us on. Bishop Jacques-Bénigne Bossuet (d. 1704) says that, out of that great and terrible wreck in which human reason lost the truth for which God had formed it, the human mind nonetheless retained a vague and uneasy desire to recover some vestiges of that truth.[4] In fact, no feeling has a stronger hold on human nature than this desire for "something new." As the poet Cesare Pavese (d. 1950) puts it, "What man looks for in pleasure is an infinite, and no one would ever give up hope of reaching this infinite."[5] Our hearts will not rest until the Infinite comes close to us. We need to be able to walk with the Infinite as a companion, and to embrace the Infinite as a friend.

Every human longing and heartache has become flesh in the Incarnation of Jesus Christ. God breaks through the desolation and inertia of the world, not with an idea or a doctrine, but with a presence in the flesh. In the midst of our barren and anguishing hearts, God places a new beginning, which is a pure gift from above.

"At the Annunciation," Blessed John Paul II tells us, "… an interior space was reopened with-

in humanity which the eternal Father" intends to
" 'fill with every spiritual blessing.' "[6] The Blessed
Virgin Mary remains forever at the heart of that
re-creation. For in conceiving Jesus, Mary became in some way the source of that grace which
the Lord was to pour forth over all mankind (St.
Thomas Aquinas).[7] Christianity is itself an annunciation, and its method is revealed in the
Annunciation: God comes to us through an encounter.

NOVENA PRAYER

*Lord Jesus, we need a hope that goes beyond all
worldly hopes. Our hearts yearn for something
more than what we can attain. Only something
infinite can satisfy our boundless longing. In the
midst of human weakness and powerlessness, you
come in the flesh. Through this mystery of divine
self-giving you reveal us to ourselves. Without you
we cannot be fully human. Thank you for the gift
of your saving Presence.*

*Please continue to draw close to us through the
Blessed Virgin Mary and to show yourself to us in
ways we can perceive. Help us feel and judge how
much you love us. As we received you, the Author
of salvation, through the "yes" of Mary, may we
continue to receive Our Lady's help toward our*

salvation in the same manner. United with the intercession of the Mother of God, I offer you these intentions: (mention your request here).

March

PALM SUNDAY OF THE PASSION OF THE LORD

WE WANT TO LIVE HOLY WEEK unlike any other week of the year. The liturgies of Holy Week provide the clue for how we can do this in the repeated reading of the Passion (today and on Good Friday). Jesus lets evil push him to the place of ultimate hate: the cross. Christ goes freely to Calvary, his heart burning with love for his Father. What stings our heart is to hear Jesus' cry from the cross: "My God, my God, why have you forsaken me?" (Mt 27:46, NABRE). St. John of the Cross (d. 1591) comments that, at that moment, Jesus was completely annihilated in his soul, bereft of any consolation or relief, "since the Father left him that way in innermost aridity." But from this experience of "the most extreme abandonment," Jesus "accomplished the most marvelous work of his whole life" — the reconciliation of the human race with God.[8]

The word "why" in Christ's cry most accurately means, "*For what reason* have you forsaken me?" The word presumes a *purpose* behind his forsakenness. Jesus asks "why," not to contest his forsakenness, but to be better able to obey the Father's plan in it. He wants to make this forsakenness part of his self-offering to the Father. Christ's forsakenness teaches us that God desires to bind us to himself in the knowledge of how lost we would be without him. "The more we approach the pure center of naked poverty," writes Father Hans Urs von Balthasar (d. 1988), "the more intimately do we take possession of ourselves, the more reliably are all things our own…. Blessed are not the enlightened whose every question has been answered and who are delighted with their own sublime light…. Blessed, rather, are the chased, the harassed who must daily stand before [God's] enigmas and cannot solve them."[9]

Thus, we need at times to feel "rejected" by God in order to open our hearts more to God's love. As St. John of the Cross puts it: "When [we are] brought to nothing … the spiritual union between [our] soul and God will be effected."[10] The Church prays, "When your heart is torn with grief, the Lord is near you."[11] With such confidence we live our Holy Week.

Novena Prayer

Loving Father, let me enter into this Holy Week deeply united with Jesus, our Redeemer. Your beloved Son willingly goes to his Passion with the full engagement of his freedom out of love for you. Allow me to share in that love. May no revilement, persecution, or betrayal keep me from handing myself over to you in confident faith. The mystery of Christ's Passion reveals that forsakenness is a grace. From the experience of extreme abandonment, Jesus reconciled the human race.

May I be strengthened to take up every cross of life without ever doubting or losing trust. You desire to bind me to yourself in the knowledge of how lost I would be without you. Bring me to a sense of nothingness to make my union with you more perfect. United with Jesus Christ, Savior of the world, I entrust to you these, my intentions: (mention your request here).

March

Chrism Mass

The celebration of the Chrism Mass (normally on Thursday of Holy Week) commemorates the anniversary of that day when Christ conferred his priesthood on his apostles. A priest is "configured in a special way" to Jesus Christ and lives as "a continuation of Christ himself…. Priests are called to prolong the presence of Christ" in the world, "embodying his way of life, and making him visible."[12] A man hands over his humanity to Christ so that the Lord will make him into "another Christ." Jesus uses the priest as an instrument of salvation. At his hands the priest gives people the Redeemer in person. The priest is consecrated to perpetuate the Holy Sacrifice, and through the Eucharist the priest manifests his true identity.

The first task of priests is to preach the Gospel, by which he generates others, mediating a saving encounter with Jesus Christ. The priest possesses and passes on the knowledge of God, which is his own personal and living experience of the Mystery. The priest exists as a "sign" and conduit "of God's merciful love for the sinner" (CCC 1465). For this reason, as Blessed John Paul II taught,

> [every] priest needs to develop and sharpen his human sensitivity so as to understand more clearly [people's] needs, respond to their demands, perceive their unvoiced questions, and share their hopes and expectations … joys and burdens. All the difficult

circumstances which people find in their path … [must be] fraternally lived and sincerely suffered in the priest's heart.

People need to come out of their anonymity and fear. They need to be known and called by name … [they need] to be found again if they have become lost, to be loved…. All this is done by Jesus the good shepherd … and by his priests with him.[13]

In the expression of the great patron of all priests, St. John Vianney (d. 1859), the priesthood is the love of the heart of Jesus. The priest's role, wrote Servant of God Catherine de Hueck Doherty (d. 1985), is "to show us the tenderness of Christ, his compassion, and his mercy. This is what will protect the Church. This is what will bring about its rebirth."[14]

NOVENA PRAYER

Loving Father, thank you for the gift of the priesthood. The sacrament of Holy Orders confers upon your priests sacramental grace. It gives them a share not only in Jesus' saving power and ministry but also in his pastoral love. Let that love grow. Allow all priests to have a deep intimacy with your

Son, especially through their devotion to the Eucharist. Deepen their configuration to Christ, and make them true fathers.

May your priests be men of integrity who love the truth, are respectful to every person, and are genuinely compassionate and deeply happy. Enable priests to know the depths of the human heart, to perceive difficulties and problems, to make encounter and dialogue easy, and to create trust and cooperation. Purify, sanctify, and renew all priests, especially those facing trouble in their vocation. United with the Blessed Virgin Mary, Mother of Priests, I offer you these intentions: (mention your request here).

March

Holy Thursday

On this night, "sacrifice" is redefined forever. At the Lord's Supper, Jesus reveals sacrifice to be not about "giving up" things so much as it is about *receiving*. "Sacrifice," writes Pope Benedict XVI, "consists in becoming totally receptive towards God and letting ourselves be completely taken over by him."[15] Sacrifice begins with the awareness that I need something more than myself in order to gain life's fulfillment. As Jesus stands before us, wrapped in an apron, holding pitcher and basin, our heart leaps: this self-emptying love is the Something Greater we seek. Sacrifice means putting aside my pride, my resistance, and my self-reliance, and letting Jesus wash my feet. That encounter with divine love incarnate is death to the false self.

While we are still awestruck at such mercy, Jesus takes up bread and wine and says, "This is my Body. This is my Blood, given for you." "We draw life from [Christ's] flesh just as he draws life from the Father" (St. Hilary of Poitiers).[16] At Mass we pray, "All my life is yours, and so I cry to you, receive it, take it. Because we do not change our own lives; they are changed by the mystery of Christ at work in us" (Luigi Giussani)[17] — for the love Jesus gives us in the Eucharist is not sentiment but rather his very *self*. With his own flesh, in an act that anticipates the Passion, Jesus sums up the meaning of human existence: to consume oneself for something. We respond by consuming him in Holy Communion. Our participation in the sacrifice of the Eucharist identifies us with Christ's heart (see CCC 1419), moving us to pursue our happiness through similar, self-sacrificing love.

To enable us, Christ institutes the priesthood — men ordained to make present the Eucharistic sacrifice in our midst. Through the presence of these "other Christs," we see the One who stooped to wash our feet. That memory penetrates all we love, purifying it so that we can love others with Christ's own love. It makes us desire to become totally receptive toward Jesus, who promises through the priest, "This is my Body. Your sins are forgiven." This is sacrifice.

Novena Prayer

Lord Jesus, on Holy Thursday night you forever re-define the meaning of sacrifice. As you kneel down to wash our feet, you teach us that Gospel sacrifice means becoming totally receptive toward God, and letting ourselves be taken over by his love. Remove all my pride and resistance. May the love I receive at your loving hands transform my life into one of generous charity toward others.

At the Last Supper, as you institute the Holy Eucharist, you give us not just your power but your very self. Thank you for this inestimable gift. May the Eucharist mold and change my life into one of constant, self-sacrificing service. In the gift of the priesthood, you bless the world with other Christs who show that you are always close, eager to forgive, instruct, and sanctify us. United with you, the Great High Priest, I offer these intentions: (mention your request here).

March

GOOD FRIDAY OF THE PASSION OF THE LORD

ON GOOD FRIDAY we want to console Jesus Christ as he dies on the cross. But how? Not through outpourings of emotion, even well-meaning ones. The purpose of Jesus in his suffering and dying is not to draw our sympathy to him. Rather, he goes to the cross in order *to give himself to us* in mercy. For this reason, the most fitting way to console Jesus on Good Friday is by disposing ourselves more and more *to receive his love.*

True love always seeks to give the loved one what he or she in fact wishes to receive. Our sentimental "feeling sorry" for Jesus is not what the Lord wants. What Christ crucified desires is for us to confess our need for a Savior. He asks us to acknowledge our sins — especially the sin of trying to be completely self-sufficient and of refusing to recognize our own limits. He begs us to admit our hopelessness in ourselves to overcome our sins, and in that knowledge of our misery, to unite ourselves with him — because he is the Answer.

We console Jesus Christ on the cross by being willing to receive his love. Jesus crucified loves us by forgiving us and purifying us. Without this scandalous innovation of love, we would go on doubting God. Blessed John Paul II says that "if the agony of the cross had not happened, the truth that God is Love would have been unfounded."[18] "By his wounds you have been healed" (1 Pt 2:24). Pope Benedict XVI tells us that the cross "is that form of love which has totally accepted human beings to the point of descending even into our guilt and death…. What looks down at us from the cross is a goodness that enables a new beginning in the midst of life's horror."[19]

The culminating point of our Good Friday worship is the moment we come forward to venerate the cross of our Redeemer. Our kiss tells Jesus that he does not die in vain, because we hand over to him our sins, confessing our belief in the power of his blood to wipe them away. That humble confidence consoles him.

NOVENA PRAYER

Crucified Savior, unworthy though I am, grant that I may stand united with your Sorrowful Mother at your holy cross. It is my sins that crucify you. You have come to call sinners. You have come for me. I appeal to your Precious Blood. Pride makes me deny my sins and keeps me locked up in guilt and shame. Help me to give myself to you just the way I am. I confess that your love for me is greater than any evil I could ever commit.

Tender Jesus, you do not die in vain! May I dwell in the wound of your pierced side, for by your wounds I am healed. As you look down from the cross, may your gaze of love bring forth a new beginning in the midst of life's horror. United with Our Lady of Compassion, I offer you my intentions: (mention your request here).

March

HOLY SATURDAY

IN THE CLOSING PRAYER of the Good Friday service, the priest prays that abundant blessing might descend on God's people who have honored the death of his Son in the hope of their resurrection. On Holy Saturday, we live out that hope in prayerful vigilance. Pope Benedict XVI tells us in his encyclical on hope that what distinguishes Christians is the fact that we have a future; we know with certainty that our "life will not end in emptiness."[20] That certainty comes from something already given to us in the present: the knowledge that we are definitively loved and that, no matter what happens to us, we are "awaited by this Love."[21]

Our life, even despite all its failures and betrayals, is held firm by that indestructible power of Love which has pity on our nothingness. The reason we have hope, says St. Thomas Aquinas (d. 1274), is that we belong to God and we know it. In fact, the very design of the human heart prompts us to hope, even amidst all the terrible difficulties we experience daily. Our heart remains driven toward an Ultimate Something, and even when we do not know what that something is, we cannot stop reaching out for it. It is hope that drives us.[22] Hope is the fulfillment of what we are made for. Yet we can ignore, or reduce, or anesthetize the demands of our heart. The resultant sins against hope, explains St. Thomas, are more dangerous than sins against faith or charity, for when hope dies we lose heart and flounder in wickedness.[23]

To live in vigilant Gospel hope, we must keep in mind that hope is not directed toward a change in our circumstances but rather toward the possibility *of our being changed* within those circumstances. Hope is asking in faith that the merciful love which was given to us today might embrace us again tomorrow. And we beg also for the grace to say yes to it. "When I am in endless darkness, so much so that I cannot stand myself anymore, it is there that I am forced to go to the bottom of it and recognize an Other" (Julián Carrón).[24]

NOVENA PRAYER

Loving Father, even in the midst of the blinding darkness that falls upon the earth at the death of your divine Son, I cannot give in to despair. And the silence that enshrouds the guilty world still resounds with every promise made by our loving Savior. Strengthen me with a hope that exceeds my sorrow. May this hope give me the capacity to confront the future with clarity and strength, and to overcome every temptation of pain, of weariness, of doubt, and of disappointment — for without hope, bitterness prevails, and we are left with the scourge of defeat, with feelings of jealousy, rivalry, and division.

As I keep vigil at the tomb of your Son, I am filled with unshakeable certainty because I know that I am awaited by an indestructible Love. United in faith with the Sorrowful Mother of God, I offer you my intentions: (mention your request here).

APRIL

April

Easter Sunday of the Resurrection of the Lord

Msgr. Luigi Giussani (d. 2005) sums up the glory of Easter: "The Resurrection of Christ means that we are no longer alone with our nothingness, with our frailty, with the needs of our heart. We are accompanied by Someone living now."[1] Conversely, "without Christ's Resurrection there is only one alternative: nothingness."[2] One outstanding "proof" of the Resurrection is the perseverance and the unity of the Church. Msgr. Giussani observes,

> Today only one great prodigy has taken the place of the original routine miracles and signs. It is the miracle of our adherence as people to the reality of that Man of 2000 years ago…. It is the event by which Christ makes himself present, in the weakness, fear, timidity, and confusion of our persons in unity.[3]

Another "proof" is the preaching of the apostles. Pope Benedict XVI wonders: What explains the boldness and passion with which the formerly cowardly apostles preached? It would be unthinkable unless they "had experienced a real encounter, coming to them from ... the self-rev-elation ... of the risen Christ."[4] His "Resurrection *abides* and draws everything toward life" (CCC 1085, emphasis in original).

Even when the nothingness of life torments us, the risen Christ always finds a way to break through. Pope Benedict XVI promises, "Christ strode through the gate of our final loneliness; in his Passion he went down into the abyss of our abandonment. Where no voice can reach us any longer, there is he."[5] And that voice says,

> Seek the things of heaven, because I am reborn. Do not look for me among the dead.... Do not wait for the end of your trials; only wait until you conquer them victoriously. Do not seek me among your regrets, among the ruins of your human hopes.... Have confidence. I have con-quered the world; and by your faith you too will conquer it; but do not expect to master it; do not expect what I have not promised: honors and an easy life. No, I have prom-ised you my help, my very life, to sanctify you.... I myself will uphold you in all your trials.... I ask you not to tarry in this pas-sageway; place your hopes higher (Mother Marie des Douleurs).[6]

NOVENA PRAYER

Risen Savior, by the power of your blessed resurrection, you have set us free and made all things new. No longer are we alone with our nothingness, our frailty, or the needs of our heart. Like the disciples with whom you walked on the road to Emmaus, you accompany us with your Risen Life. May the grace of your resurrection change and perfect me in holiness.

When the events of life lead me to the abyss of unbearable loneliness and to the brink of despair, come to me in an encounter that surpasses all I can imagine. Where no voice can reach us, you speak our name. Your resurrection empowers us with a new capacity to love and fills us with joy. May your risen Presence shine in all relationships once ruled by fear and doubt. Exulting in the Easter Alleluia, I offer you my intentions: (mention your request here).

April

DIVINE MERCY SUNDAY

THE SECOND SUNDAY of Easter is known as Divine Mercy Sunday. This feast was established in recognition of the life and the writings of

St. Faustina Kowalska (d. 1938), known as the apostle of Divine Mercy. In a homily, Blessed John Paul II — who canonized her — quoted our Lord's words to the saint: " 'Humanity will never find peace until it turns with trust to Divine Mercy.' … Divine Mercy! This is the Easter gift that the Church receives from the risen Christ and offers to humanity."[7] This day "concentrates on the mercy poured forth in Christ's Death and Resurrection, fount of the Holy Spirit who forgives sins and restores joy at having been redeemed."[8]

Mercy is the fact of God's preference for us in the face of all our real wretchedness, evildoing, and betrayal. It is the love the Father offers us precisely at the moment when we deserve it the least — given simply because God is good, and not because we are. Mercy brings us face-to-face with the fact of our nothingness. Before God created the world, there was nothing. The theologian Josef Pieper (d. 1997), calling upon the authority of St. Thomas Aquinas, explains that our descent from nothing is the deepest ground for the human being's capacity for sin. Since we come from nothing, it is inherent to the will not to remain in the good by nature.[9]

Yet, the memory of our origin from nothing brings us certainty about God's mercy. For the quality of mercy consists in bringing a thing out of nonbeing into being (St. Thomas Aquinas).[10]

We are made by mercy that loves us into existence — and continues to recreate us. Pope John Paul II assures us, "Evil can be overcome if we open ourselves to [the love of God to the point of contempt of self]. This is the fruit of Divine Mercy. In Jesus Christ, God bends down over man to hold out a hand to him, to raise him up, and to help him continue his journey with renewed strength."[11]

NOVENA PRAYER

Loving Savior, have mercy on me, according to your own immense, incomprehensible mercy — a mercy that exceeds all my sins put together. Humanity will never find peace until it turns with trust to Divine Mercy. Save me from the blackmail of sin that leads me to deny the existence of sin, to deny the reality of my own sins, to make excuses or to blame others for my sins, or to try to make reparation for my sins without recourse to Divine Mercy.

Do not let me be despondent over my nothingness, but rather let me use that self-knowledge to turn to you in confidence. Jesus, I trust in you! Recreate me in the mercy that made me. Rescue those caught in the snare of sin. Increase my desire and my ability to show mercy to others. United in your mercy, I offer you my intentions: (make your request here).

April

WORLD DAY OF PRAYER FOR VOCATIONS

ANNUALLY, on the Fourth Sunday of Easter, the Church observes the World Day of Prayer for Vocations. It first calls to mind the vocation that every human being shares. The vocation of every human being is to make visible in his or her life the image of God and to manifest that transformation of self to the world. The particular Christian vocation entails making God evident to the eyes of all by living as a witness who acts in God's image and likeness — that is, by a faith-driven life of sincere, self-giving love (see CCC 1877, 2085, 2392).

The Holy Spirit reveals and communicates to each person this fundamental and innate vocation. Dwelling within us, God's Spirit becomes the principle and wellspring of the fulfillment of our vocation. He configures us to Christ, making us sharers in his life of love — a spiritual life by which he leads us toward "the perfection of charity."[12]

One way we respond to the universal call to holiness is by helping to promote vocations (see Mt 9:38; Lk 10:2). An integral part of the Church's mission consists in proposing "clearly and courageously to each new generation the vocational call"

— helping people first "to discern the authenticity" of the personal vocation given them by God, and then "to respond to it generously."[13] As Blessed John Paul II writes: "Indeed, concern for vocations is a connatural and essential dimension of the Church's pastoral work…. In the Church's very name, *ecclesia*, we find its deep vocational aspect, for the Church is a 'convocation,' an assembly of those who have been called."[14]

The Church observes this day by concentrating on vocations to the ordained ministries (priesthood and diaconate), to the religious and consecrated life in all its forms (male and female, contemplative and apostolic), to societies of apostolic life, to secular institutes, and to the missionary life. "Of its very nature priesthood is a reply to the insistent, profound, fundamental questions asked by man about the meaning of the whole of reality. The priest … expresses this meaning and … conveys it to the world."[15] And "it is the duty of the *consecrated life* to show that the Incarnate Son of God is … the infinite beauty which alone can fully satisfy the human heart."[16]

Novena Prayer

Loving Father, I thank you for the vocation you give every human being to show forth the image of God through a life of self-sacrificing love. Thank you for the particular vocation you have given me. Your Son commanded us to pray to the Lord of the harvest to send out laborers into his harvest. We do that now. At every moment, we seek the face of your Son, and we find his presence in priests ordained to be other Christs and in consecrated religious, whose lives reflect the infinite beauty of the Word Incarnate.

Bless the Church with many new vocations. Grant young people an attentive and generous spirit with which to listen to your Son's voice and respond in obedience. Move their hearts to heed his call and follow in freedom and joy. United with Jesus the Great High Priest, I offer my intentions: (mention your request here).

MAY

May 1

ST. JOSEPH THE WORKER

THE LITURGICAL MEMORIAL of St. Joseph the Worker was established by Pope Pius XII (d. 1958) to highlight the importance of work and of the presence of Christ and the Church in the working world. It provides an occasion to reflect on — and witness to — the "Gospel of work." In a particular way, St. Joseph, the carpenter of Nazareth, stands as patron of workers and craftsmen, revered as a singular model. Blessed John Paul II, in his encyclical on human work, encourages us to live with the awareness that "work is a participation in God's activity" — an awareness that "ought to permeate … even '*the most ordinary everyday activities.*' " By our labor and personal industry, we "are unfolding the Creator's work … and contributing to 'the realization in history of the divine plan.' "[1]

Work positively affects the worker's family, the whole of society, and the worker personally. "It forms the person in the process of transforming things; it humanizes and spiritualizes the person in the process of modifying material objects. And finally, it draws men together in the pursuit of a goal that is visible to all, and in the construction of the world in which they are called to live"

(Louis Lavelle).[2] Thus when a worker offers to God not only the firstfruits of labor but his labor itself, human labor "can become a great liturgy of worship" (M. D. Philippe).[3]

For this reason, Msgr. Lorenzo Albacete calls work a "spiritual act":

It is only by confronting the daily demands of work that we deepen our interior dynamism.... Work itself is meant to become a spiritual act, and this happens when it is experienced as being at the service of the quest for the Infinite. We are often called upon to do "mindless" work. But our spiritual task is to transform it. Emptying the trash can be considered mindless, but if I see it as a contribution to the well-being of my family, it can be immensely significant for me.[4]

For Christianity, then, "human work represents the gradual beginnings of man's dominion over things, of a governance to which he aspires by realizing the image of God" (Luigi Giussani).[5]

NOVENA PRAYER

Glorious St. Joseph, in your diligent daily labor, you provided for the household of the Holy Family.

Patron of all workers, you model how work is a participation in God's own activity. Our Lord Jesus Christ declared, "My food is to do the will of him who sent me, and to accomplish his work" (Jn 4:34). I pray for the sanctification of all human labor. Through it, God never ceases to perfect and govern the immense work of creation.

We are called to contribute by our diligent industry to the unfolding of the Creator's plan in history. Protect the rights of all workers. Enable people to find work that befits their dignity. Do not let those who are unemployed become discouraged, but aid them in finding fitting jobs. May I approach my work as an act of worship. United in your powerful intercession, I offer you my intentions: (mention your request here).

May 31

THE VISITATION OF THE BLESSED VIRGIN MARY

THE MYSTERY OF THE VISITATION is a microcosm of the Christian life. The Mother of God journeying with Jesus in her womb to her kinswoman Elizabeth is the first *Corpus Christi* procession. Mary brings to us the nearness of God made flesh, carrying out an integral role in communicating the Blessed Trinity to humankind. We are made for this presence alive in the tabernacle of Mary's body. Our Lady desires to generate in us the bond of love she shares with her Son.

John the Baptist's leaping in his mother's womb mirrors our joy at being in Christ's Eucharistic Presence. "*Mary constantly sets before [us] the 'mysteries' of her Son, with the desire that the contemplation of those mysteries will release their saving power*" (Blessed John Paul II).[6] We are struck by the divine mercy infusing this mystery. God comes to us on his own initiative without waiting for us to ask him. He seeks us out. Bishop Bossuet makes the point that our Lord intentionally hides his power in the Visitation to show how he is the invisible force moving all things. The holy union that God forms with us, and his secret way of visiting us, is one of the greatest glories of Christianity.[7]

At the same time, the real unworthiness we experience because of human sinfulness, voiced by Elizabeth, gives way to the graces borne to us by Mary. As St. Louis de Montfort (d. 1716) counsels, "The Blessed Virgin will fill you with great confidence in God and in herself because you no longer approach Jesus Christ by your own self, but always through this good Mother."[8] Mary's attestation to God's greatness in the *Magnificat* (see Lk 1:46-55) is verified in the Beatitudes: God looks with favor on Mary's lowliness, and Jesus calls the meek blessed; God promises mercy on those who fear him, and Jesus declares, "Blessed are the merciful"; God has lifted up the lowly, and Jesus promises, "Blessed are the poor in spirit"; God has filled the hungry with good things, and Jesus proclaims, "Blessed are those who hunger and thirst for righteousness" (Mt 5:3-7). The Scriptural basis for the phenomenon of Marian apparitions is the Visitation.

Novena Prayer

Immaculate Mother of God, you carry in your blessed womb the only joy of every human heart. You bear to us the very nearness of God in the flesh. Come close to me in my longing. Set before me the mysteries of your divine Son. May their saving power be released in my life through my devout union with you. I beg to share in the bond of love you live with Jesus.

You always seek us out. Like the blessed Elizabeth, may I ever be prompt and eager to welcome you into my heart. In humility, I acknowledge my own nothingness and unworthiness. Through companionship with you, the lowly are lifted up. You teach us to live our faith as a demanding and engaging journey that calls for courage and constant perseverance. Filled with confidence through my union with you, I offer you my intentions: (mention your request here).

May

The Ascension of the Lord

As the disciples witnessed the stunning sight of Jesus ascending from their midst corporally (see Acts 1:9), their question must have been: What now? Without doubt the event moved them to reflect on how much their lives had changed since meeting Jesus Christ and living day after day in his physical presence. With the Ascension, would it all be over? No, for the Lord had commanded them to "wait for the promise of the Father" (Acts 1:4). And the promise of the Father always takes the form of a new way of being loved.

St. Augustine (d. 430) recognizes the need for the Ascension by simply acknowledging a fact of human experience. As long as Christ continued to dwell among them, the thoughts of the disciples would remain focused on "the Man Jesus

… unable to give their minds to God." But "if the Man should be withdrawn from their eyes and from among them, then they would think of his divinity." St. Augustine imagines Jesus saying: "Let my mortal body be raised up to heaven that you may learn what you are to hope for."[9]

In fact, as St. Leo the Great comments: "[The Son of God] now began to be indescribably more present in his divinity to those from whom he was further removed in his humanity."[10] Pope Benedict XVI develops this further:

> "Ascension" does not mean departure into a remote region of the cosmos but, rather, the continuing closeness that the disciples experience so strongly that it becomes a source of lasting joy…. Now … through his power over space, he is present and accessible to all — throughout history and in every place.[11]

Even more, Jesus' ascension into heaven redefines the very notion of "heaven." Pope Benedict XVI says that heaven is not a place but a person — the person in whom God and human beings are forever, inseparably one. And since Jesus himself is what we call "heaven," we enter into heaven to the extent that we go to Jesus and live united with him as he participates in the Father's royal power. "In this sense, 'ascension into heaven' can be something that takes place in our everyday lives."[12]

NOVENA PRAYER

Lord Jesus, as you are lifted from our sight at the Ascension, you lift up our hearts. You make it possible for us to set our eyes and minds on the higher things of heaven. You love us in a new way. Outwardly you withdraw from us, but inwardly you fill us with yourself. It is in your divinity that you take possession of our souls.

Be ever more present to me with your divine life. Dwell within me that I may be inwardly changed and given a share in your heavenly glory. Free me from all undue attachments that keep me from living in the truth. On this day, you teach us what we are to hope for. May the Ascension grace of your continuing closeness be for me a source of lasting joy. As you intercede before the Father, I offer you my intentions: (mention your request here).

JUNE

June

PENTECOST

PENTECOST IS A KIND OF CHRISTMAS. God rejoices to give himself to us. With the sending of the Holy Spirit, the Blessed Trinity is fully revealed to the world. The Holy Spirit continues to make Jesus Christ tangibly present in the Church. Through the Spirit's inner presence, all that Jesus taught and gave to us becomes more and more our own. At the same time, the Holy Spirit frees us from our creaturely limits and renders us capable of receiving God, "responding to him … knowing him, and … loving him far beyond [our] own natural capacity" (CCC 52). The Holy Spirit interiorly perfects our spirit, communicating to it a new dynamism so that it refrains from evil for love (St. Thomas Aquinas).[1] The Holy Spirit purifies us of everything in us that is not Jesus, disposing us to receive the fullness of his divine life.

The Consoler convinces the world concerning sin (see Jn 16:8) — he shows us the evil that sin contains. We cannot grasp this without the Spirit of Truth's light. In order to attain to the remedy of forgiveness, says St. Leo the Great, we need the tears of repentance that come from the Comforter.[2] Fittingly does the Holy Spirit appear as fire, notes St. Gregory the Great (d. 604), because in every heart he enters he drives out the torpor of coldness and kindles the desire for eternity.[3] He draws near to a soul through the withdrawal of the passions that formerly kept one alienated from God (St. Basil).[4] In wiping away our iniquity, the Spirit uplifts to the highest dignity those who had been betrayed by their own sins (St. John Chrysostom).[5]

The Spirit enables us to understand our own humanity in a new way. In the gift of the Spirit's Person, Christians are blessed with a new personality. The Spirit so transforms those in whom he chooses to dwell that they begin to live a completely new kind of life: "It is quite natural … for cowards to become [people] of great courage" (St. Cyril of Alexandria).[6] The visible unity of the Church is both the work and the living proof of the Holy Spirit.

NOVENA PRAYER

O Holy Spirit, you come with the tenderness of a true friend. You come as a protector to save, to heal, to teach, to counsel, to strengthen, and to console. Come and be with me. Teach me what I must do and how I must act so that I may please you in all things. Touch my heart with your love. Help me to see things beyond the range of human vision. Let me live in true humility so that you may find me capable of receiving you.

The greater a person's desire to be worthy of you, the fuller is your presence in that one's soul. Join me to yourself with your sevenfold gifts. Grant me the grace to grasp hidden things. Enlighten me so that I may become spiritual myself and able to radiate your grace to others. Divine Paraclete, I offer you my intentions: (mention your request here).

June

THE MOST HOLY TRINITY

THE CREATOR LOOKS AT ADAM in the Garden of Eden and says, "It is not good that the man should be alone" (Gn 2:18). The human being is made in the image and likeness of God; it is not good for man to be alone because God himself is not "alone." The *Catechism of the Catholic Church* tells us that " 'God is one, but not solitary' (*Fides Damasi*: DS 71)" (CCC 254). He would be, says St. Thomas Aquinas, were there not a plurality of persons in the divine nature.[7] God's "innermost secret," revealed through the Incarnation, is that he "is an eternal exchange of love, Father, Son, and Holy Spirit, and he has destined us to share in that exchange" (CCC 221).

The way God is as Trinity is the way we need to be loved by God: a Father who reveals that our origin is Love; a Son who makes us brothers and sisters; the Spirit who sanctifies the spiritual aspect of our self. The revelation of God as Father makes our heart exult, filling us with certainty: *I do not come from myself — before all else I am a child; through the love of the Father I become myself.* The truth of the Father is revealed in the Son. "Christ's whole earthly life — his words and deeds, his silences ... indeed his manner of being and speaking," teaches the *Catechism*, "... is *Revelation* of the Father" (CCC 516, emphasis in original).

Jesus lives to transform us into the Father's adopted sons and daughters: "To all who received him ... he gave power to become children of God" (Jn 1:12). We know he can because, as Jesus lives among us, he forgives our sins — something only God can do. That is the love we need from the Son of God. It is given not as a sentiment but as a divine Person: the Holy Spirit, who, when sent into our hearts, makes us cry out, "Abba! Father!" (Gal 4:6).

The Blessed Trinity, then, is the definitive answer to human loneliness. Because God is Father, we know that we belong to Someone. Because he is Son, we are blessed with a brother, a companion, and a friend — who, when he loves us, saves us — unceasingly showing us the Father (see Jn 14:9). And because he is Holy Spirit, no longer are we alone, even with our thoughts, our feelings, our emotions, or even our personality — the Holy Spirit is closer to us than our own spirit is to ourselves.

Novena Prayer

Most Blessed Trinity, to be human is to yearn for the all-embracing meaning of life. I am not the measure of my longings. I must look beyond myself. You are what makes life worth living — for you are an eternal exchange of love, and you destine me to share in that exchange.

As Father, you reveal my deepest truth: I am part of a belonging. Father, your love makes me to be myself — makes me your child. You send your Son to fulfill the constant yearning of the human heart: "Show us the Father!" The Incarnation of the Word blesses us with a companion and brother who reveals that to be human is to live in holy dependence and in obedience to your will. Your Holy Spirit is the forgiveness that heals and restores us to your friendship. Through Christ our Lord, I offer you my intentions: (mention request here).

June

THE MOST HOLY BODY AND BLOOD OF CHRIST

THE WORLD FOREVER CHANGED that Holy Thursday night when, at the Last Supper, our Lord Jesus Christ instituted the Holy Eucharist. Up to that moment, the human race had lived like the leper: abject in his misery, yet driven with expectation of the day when One would appear to whom he would declare: "If you wish, you can make me clean" (Mk 1:40, NABRE). Never could the leper have imagined the cure for his flesh to be Flesh.

So immense is the miracle of the Eucharist that we require a separate occasion on which to celebrate and contemplate it. Through our observance of the liturgical feast of *Corpus Christi*, we profess that the holiness God has destined for us is to be found in the humanity of Christ. And we fly to it like the woman in the Gospel, infirm from a twelve-year flow of blood (see Mk 5:25-34). The failure of worldly know-how to remedy her disease only increases the woman's resolve to lay hold of her healing in something beyond. Like her, our life is about finding and touching Jesus Christ, because we know that if we do so, we will be made whole. What the hemorrhaging woman seeks in Jesus is not a message but a presence.

That is why, at the Last Supper, our Lord leaves us not a book, but his own Body. In the Eucharist, Christ hands over to us his very *self*. For without the self of Jesus Christ in the Eucharist — Body, Blood, soul, and divinity — we would wander the world in a vain attempt to recover the love we had once experienced in all the places where we had encountered him. But instead, we go forth into the world in Eucharistic procession, bearing to those in need of healing the One who healed us.

Our worship of this Sacrament saves us from endless disintegration. In adoration, we beg Jesus Christ that his most holy Body and Blood will free us from all our sins, will guard us from every evil, will keep us faithful to his commandments, and will never let us be parted from him.

NOVENA PRAYER

Loving Father, you are the King who prepares a wedding banquet for his Son and invites all his servants to be his guests. At the Last Supper, your Son becomes our Host. Make me totally receptive to this incomparable Sacrifice and completely taken over by it. We are made for this Real Presence. The miracle of the Eucharist enables us to overcome our own deficiency. "What has passed our lips as food, O Lord, / may we possess in purity of heart."[8] Nourished with the Body of Christ, your people become the Body of Christ.

May the all-surpassing love of Holy Communion draw others into communion with you. Let me more and more adore the Body, Blood, soul, and divinity of your Son in the Blessed Sacrament. May the Bread of Life "given to us in time ... be our healing for eternity."[9] In Eucharistic thanksgiving, I offer you my intentions: (mention your request here).

June

THE MOST SACRED HEART OF JESUS

"THE TERM 'SACRED HEART OF JESUS,' " states the *Directory on Popular Piety and the Liturgy*, "denotes the entire mystery of Christ."[10] This feast, observed on the Friday following the second Sunday after Pentecost, is an occasion to celebrate *that* God loves us, *how* he loves us, and *what* our response to such love should be. St. Claude de la Colombière (d. 1682), promoter of devotion to the Sacred Heart, tells us that the principal virtues we honor in the Sacred Heart are Jesus' ardent love for the Father, an extreme sorrow for the sins he took upon himself, a profound compassion for our miseries, an immense love for us in spite of all we are, and an imperturbable tranquillity of soul flowing from his perfect conformity to God's will.[11]

Our heart was made for this Heart. The Sacred Heart loves us because *he* is good — not because we are. And our Lord longs for us mystically to share his Sacred Heart: "The supreme longing of Jesus' Sacred Heart is that he should be admitted, not merely to the throne of the heart or to the tribunal of conscience, but to that inner secret chamber of the soul where a man is most himself, and therefore most utterly alone" (Robert Hugh Benson).[12]

Through our recourse to the Sacred Heart, we can conquer our enemies and obtain the strength and consolation we need. So teaches St. Margaret Mary Alocoque, the seventeenth-century French nun to whom our Lord confided the mission of establishing devotion to his Sacred Heart: "If you are submerged in the waters of infidelity and inconstancy, plunge yourself into the fathomless deep of the Sacred Heart. Its stability and steadfastness will teach you to be faithful to him … as he has ever been in his love for us."[13] Pope Benedict XVI counsels that even our shortcomings, our limitations, and our weaknesses must lead us back to the Heart of Jesus. For "God's heart calls to our hearts, inviting us to come out of ourselves, to forsake our human certainties, to trust in him, and by following his example, to make ourselves a gift of unbounded love."[14]

Novena Prayer

O Sacred Heart of Jesus, I love you and I want to love you more. The heart is the dwelling place where I live — always remain close to me. The heart is my hidden center, the place to which I withdraw — when I am lonely, or worried, or overcome with sorrow, let me know the comfort of your presence.

The heart is the place of decision, the place of truth, where we choose life or death — enable me always to live in the truth. May I be completely devoted to God's will. The heart is the place of encounter, the place of covenant — please allow nothing but you and my relationship with you to be the measure of my life. Enlarge my heart and make me generous in charity toward others, especially the poor. With confidence in your tender, boundless love, I offer you these, my intentions: (mention your request here).

June

THE IMMACULATE HEART OF THE BLESSED VIRGIN MARY

THE MEMORIAL of the Immaculate Heart of Mary falls on the day after the solemnity of the Sacred Heart of Jesus. Commenting on these tandem liturgical feasts, the *Directory on Popular Piety and the Liturgy* states:

> The contiguity of both celebrations is in itself a liturgical sign of their close connection: the *mysterium* of the Heart of Jesus is projected onto and reverberates in the Heart of his Mother ... the memorial of the Immaculate Heart of Mary [celebrates] the complex visceral relationship of Mary with her Son's work of salvation.[15]

St. John Eudes (d. 1680), the great promoter of devotion to the Immaculate Heart of Mary, says that Jesus poured into the heart of his mother the plenitude of the treasures of wisdom and knowledge hidden in his own heart.[16]

We see the love of the Immaculate Heart of Mary dramatized throughout the Gospel. Mary's love given at the Visitation represents the Blessed

Virgin's desire to mediate God's mercy, to lift up
the lowly, and to fill the hungry with good things,
as Our Lady sings in her *Magnificat*. In the midst
of the world's menacing darkness, coldness, and
rejection, Mary gives birth to the Son of God and
beckons us to discover in her arms the Answer
to the longing of our heart. Mary's immaculate
love constantly anticipates and provides for every human need by entrusting our want to her
Son, as Our Lady does when she intercedes at the
wedding feast of Cana. And as Christ's heart is
pierced on Calvary, so too is his mother's heart
mystically pierced so that Mary can accompany
us in our sufferings with the divine love un-
leashed through those open wounds.

United with the Immaculate Heart of Mary,
we can love Jesus Christ with the love with which
he deserves to be loved. We venerate the Immaculate Heart of Mary because at the heart of that
Heart is Jesus Christ. If we love the love Mary offers us through her Immaculate Heart, then "the
Mother of God will open your heart and make
it big and generous in running in the way of the
commandments" (St. Louis de Montfort).[17]

Novena Prayer

Glorious Virgin Mary, I long to love your Son, Je-
sus, the way he deserves to be loved — with the

love of your Immaculate Heart. Unite me to your Immaculate Heart so that I will be open to receive your Son with the same dispositions by which you received him. Your Immaculate Heart is supremely gentle, steadfast, watchful — completely given over to the will of God. Lead me out of the darkness of ignorance, free me from all selfishness and willful self-assertion, and train me in conformity with your Immaculate Heart.

Let me always trust in your Immaculate Heart as a true source of grace and mercy. In sharing in the Passion of your Son, your Immaculate Heart was pierced. May your immaculate love embrace me in moments of suffering. I beg to make reparation for all offenses against your Immaculate Heart as I offer you my intentions: (mention your request here).

June 24

THE NATIVITY OF ST. JOHN THE BAPTIST

APART FROM THE NATIVITY OF THE LORD, the Church celebrates the nativity of only two other people: the Blessed Virgin Mary and St. John the Baptist. Since the abundant graces associated with these two holy ones arise with their

beginning, the Church directs our devotion to
their births … and even before — to their lives
in the womb!

At the Visitation, from within the womb of
his mother, Elizabeth, John the Baptist comes in
contact with Jesus present in the womb of Mary.
That encounter makes the fetal John leap for joy,
like King David dancing before the Ark of the
Covenant. The event reveals how the human
heart is made for Jesus Christ and "knows" him
through a kind of magnetic attraction — even
before the benefit of birth. Some great saints
held the belief that John the Baptist was thereby
sanctified by Christ in the womb and born without original sin. From the moment of the mysti-
cal meeting of the two mothers with their sons,
John is professing to his cousin Savior: "You are
the Lamb of God. I am not worthy to unfasten
the straps of your sandals. You must increase; I
must decrease."

At John's naming, his formerly mute father,
Zechariah, sings to his baby boy:

> "You, child, will be called the prophet of the
> Most High; for you will go before the Lord
> to prepare his ways, to give knowledge of
> salvation to his people in the forgiveness of
> their sins, …to give light to those who sit in

darkness and in the shadow of death." (Lk 1:76-77, 79)

The miracles surrounding the nativity of the Baptist make us desire to live out John's joyful attention to the presence of Jesus who always comes close to us.

The Baptist's mission moves us to be simple in acknowledging our sins and confident in seeking forgiveness, for in that confession comes "knowledge of salvation." Today is born, in the words of Jesus, "a burning and shining lamp" (Jn 5:35) — the darkness in our life does not stand a chance. In the tender compassion of our God, the Dawn from on high has broken upon us through the birth of John the Baptist.

NOVENA PRAYER

Glorious St. John, while still in the womb of your mother, Elizabeth, you leapt for joy before the presence of Jesus Christ alive in the womb of the Blessed Virgin Mary. Draw me into that encounter of sanctifying love. You were born to go before the Lord to prepare his way. May my life be like yours in humility, simplicity, and total surrender to Jesus Christ. You were born to give people knowledge of salvation by the forgiveness of their sins. Help me to know my sins and to confess them, confident in God's mercy. I must decrease; Jesus must increase.

May your announcement, pronounced before Holy Communion at Mass, "Behold, the Lamb of God" (Jn 1:29), lead me into ever deeper intimacy with Jesus in the Eucharist. Be a burning and shining lamp in my darkness. Confident in your powerful intercession, I offer to you my intentions: (mention your request here).

June 29

STS. PETER AND PAUL

Are there two people more unlike each other than Simon Peter and Paul of Tarsus? Yet we celebrate their memory together because what unites them outdistances their differences. Jesus Christ's invitation to union with himself comes while each man is mired in his own brand of resistance. After a skeptical Peter catches a miraculous draught of fish at Christ's command, he falls at the knees of Jesus saying, "Depart from me, for I am a sinful man, O Lord" (Lk 5:8). The prisoner Paul confesses to King Agrippa, "I myself was convinced that I ought to do many things in opposing the name of Jesus" (Acts 26:9), and it was when Saul was "still breathing threats and murder against the disciples of the Lord" (Acts 9:1) that Jesus appeared to him on the road to Damascus.

In the Transfiguration, Jesus shows himself to Peter like light itself, in garments "glistening, intensely white, as no fuller on earth could bleach them" (Mk 9:3). On the road, Paul testifies, "I saw on the way a light from heaven, brighter than the sun, shining round me" (Acts 26:13). To the apostle Peter, the Lord declares: "Whatever you loose on earth shall be loosed in heaven" (Mt 16:19). To the apostle Paul, the Lord reveals: "I send you to open their eyes, that they may turn from … the power of Satan to God, that they may receive forgiveness of sins" (Acts 26:17-18).

Peter three times denied knowing Jesus on the verge of the Passion (see Jn 18:17, 25, 27). Jesus asks Paul directly, "Saul, Saul, why do you persecute me?" (Acts 9:4). Peter overheard Jesus pray, "Abba, Father" (Mk 14:36). Paul teaches us to pray, "Abba! Father!" (Rom 8:15). Peter heals the lame man with the words "In the name of Jesus Christ of Nazareth, rise and walk" (Acts 3:6). Jesus pronounces Paul's mission: "To carry my name before the Gentiles and kings and the sons of Israel" (Acts 9:15).

"In Peter the weak things of the world were chosen, to confound the strong; in Paul sin abounded so that grace might abound the more. In each of them what shone forth was the great grace and glory of God, who made them deserving" (St. Augustine).[18]

NOVENA PRAYER

Glorious St. Peter and St. Paul, at a moment when you each denied Jesus Christ, the grace of God prevailed, and you became champions of the Gospel. Where sin increased, grace abounded all the more — for love covers a multitude of sins. Bless me with the strength of your faith, hope, and love. Help me to become holy in every aspect of my conduct after the likeness of the One who called me.

You accepted in your lives a sharing in the Passion of our Lord so that you might trust, not in yourselves, but in God, who raises the dead. Strengthen me to embrace the cross of Christ, and let me share your trust. By his wounds we are healed. May my life proclaim that Christ's grace is enough for me — for me to live is Christ. United in your intercession, I offer my intentions: (mention your request here).

JULY

July 1

THE MOST PRECIOUS BLOOD OF CHRIST

IN THE PRE-1969 LITURGICAL CALENDAR, July 1 was the feast of the Precious Blood of Christ. It was removed from the calendar because the Blood of Christ is already venerated in other feasts such as that of the Sacred Heart. It may still be observed, however, in a votive Mass — that is, when another Mass for that particular day is not stipulated.

We eagerly venerate this mystery for, as St. John declares, "The blood of Jesus … cleanses us from all sin" (1 Jn 1:7). The Precious Blood purifies us through our seeing, thinking, and drinking. The enslaved Hebrews in Egypt daubed blood of the Passover lamb on their doorposts as a sign to the destroying angel, who, seeing the blood, passed over the house (see Ex 12:7, 21-22). St. Clement of Rome (died c. 100) urges, "Let us look steadfastly to the blood of Christ, and see how precious that blood is to God, which, having been shed for our salvation, has set the grace of repentance before the whole world."[1] Conversely, "where demons see the blood of the Lord," comments St. John Chrysostom, "they flee, while angels gather."[2]

Moreover, St. Gregory the Great refers to the Precious Blood as "the cry of our Redeemer …

[which] has asked for, and obtained, life for his persecutors."[3] "The faithful are 'precious' because of the 'price' (*pretium*) Christ paid for them" (Raniero Cantalamessa; see Acts 20:28).[4] God the Father says, through St. Catherine of Siena (d. 1380), that he does not want souls to think about their sins without calling to mind the Precious Blood.[5] If we do, promises St. Catherine, "remembrance of the Precious Blood restores warmth and light to cold and darkened souls. It gives generosity, and frees from small-heartedness. It frees from pride, and pours in humility. It frees from cruelty, and gives compassion."[6] Confidence in this moves the sixteenth-century Jesuit poet/martyr St. Robert Southwell (d. 1595) to pray,

> Jesu, let thy blood run in my mind as a water of life to cleanse … my sins and to bring forth the fruit of life everlasting.[7]

When we reverently drink the Precious Blood in Holy Communion, as St. John Chrysostom assures us, Christ's blood "at once refreshes the soul and instills a certain great power in it…. It drives away demons and puts them at a distance from us, and even summons to us angels and the Lord of angels."[8] We "who once were far off have been brought near in the blood of Christ" (Eph 2:13).

Novena Prayer

*Lord Jesus, in your Precious Blood we have re-
demption, the forgiveness of our sins — for by
the Blood of your cross you reconcile all things to
yourself and make peace. We who were once far
off have been brought near in your Precious Blood.
Let me never go astray. Deepen my devotion to
your Precious Blood.*

*It is the Blood of Christ that can purify my inner
self. May Communion with your Precious Blood
empower me to leave behind my old self, and renounce old habits. By the strength of your Blood,
the virtues are built up within me and bring life. Let
me always be bathed in your Blood, divine Savior
— a spring of water welling up to eternal life. May I
live my faith devoutly, even to the point of shedding
my blood for the Gospel. United in your Precious
Blood, I offer my intentions: (make request here).*

July

World Youth Day

The Church celebrates World Youth Day in
order to share with the whole world the hope
of many young people who want to commit
themselves to Christ and others. What is youth?

Blessed John Paul II proposes an answer: "It is a time given by Providence to every person and given to him as a responsibility. During that time he searches, like the young man in the Gospel, for answers to basic questions; he searches not only for the meaning of life but also for a concrete way to go about living his life."[9]

Pope Benedict XVI follows through on this theme in a World Youth Day message in which he points out that "in every period of history … many young people experience a deep desire for personal relationships marked by truth and solidarity … the urge to break out of the ordinary." He writes,

> Part of being young is desiring something beyond everyday … a yearning for something really truly greater…. Men and women were created for … infinity. Nothing else will ever be enough…. The desire for a more meaningful life is a sign that God created us and that we bear his "imprint." … To set God aside is to separate ourselves from that source and, inevitably, to deprive ourselves of fulfillment and joy.[10]

And given the fact that, as St. Augustine says, "God is younger than all else," it is not at all surprising that there exists a certain spiritual youth-fulness which never grows old, despite the aging of our body. Pope John Paul II, who himself remained perpetually youthful throughout his long, saintly life, describes this in his apostolic exhortation *Vita Consecrata*: "There is a youth-fulness of spirit which lasts through time; it arises from the fact that at every stage of life a person seeks and finds a new task to fulfill, a particular way of being, of serving and of loving."[11] St. Basil, recognizing this truth himself, exclaimed: "The person who reaches out for what lies ahead of him is always becoming younger than himself."[12] No matter our age, faith moves us to be that young person. World Youth Day is for each one of us!

Novena Prayer

Most merciful Father, your beloved Son, Jesus, commands us to change and become like little children so as to enter the Kingdom of God. The Church depends on young people. She relies on their lively faith, their creative charity, and the energy of their hope. Their presence renews, rejuvenates, and gives new vigor to the Church.

Be close to young people throughout the world. Protect them in their innocence and purity. Save them from isolation and loneliness. Shelter them from the lies and deception of the world. Form them to live the life of Christ. Bless and enrich their friendships. Let them find their happiness and peace in belonging to you. Put holy adults in their lives to care for them. Move young people to make of their lives a faith-filled gift of self. With thanks for the gift of youthfulness, I offer you my intentions: (mention your request here).

AUGUST

August 6

THE TRANSFIGURATION OF THE LORD

IN ALL TRUE FRIENDSHIPS, there comes a moment when the friend wants to share what is most dear to him or her with a friend. Christ calls his closest apostles — Peter, James, and John — to a mountaintop and reveals the "secret" of himself. Jesus understands humanity's yearning for Something More — the longing to lay hold of the Infinite. What makes the adventure of life possible is the possibility of a relationship with what is beyond us. Christ confirms that today.

Bishop Massimo Camisasca says that "God wants to communicate himself through the human, and he accepts all of its ambiguities. God enters into the problematic complexity of our existence in order to make it shine transparently with his light."[1] In our search for the ultimate meaning of life, we must adhere first of all "to our own natures, and be mindful that the outcome of our search could well demand a radical change, a breaking through and beyond the limits of our own natures" (Luigi Giussani).[2]

This is the precise point of the Transfiguration. St. Leo the Great writes that through the Transfiguration "the whole body of Christ was to understand the kind of transformation that it would receive as his gift. The members of [Christ's body] were to look forward to [sharing] in that glory which first blazed out in Christ."[3] St. Thomas Aquinas adds, "Christ showed his disciples the glory of his radiance to which he configures those who are his."[4]

The Transfiguration proclaims:

> Another has become our measure…. The Mystery … wants to make Itself known, to make Itself loved in human experience…. It wants to make Itself seen in Its power and in Its glory…. Within the man to whom Christ draws near and who freely desires and accepts the relationship with him … his nature as a man changes…. Man remains man but becomes something more…. If we live [the mystery of the ecclesial community], … then we will become different in a verifiable way." (Luigi Giussani)[5]

The Byzantine Liturgy sings: "Through your Transfiguration, O Christ, you returned Adam's nature to its original splendor, restoring its very elements to the glory and brilliance of your divinity."[6]

Novena Prayer

Lord Jesus, your Transfiguration is a supreme act of friendship by which you reveal the deepest truth about yourself to your companions. In your Transfiguration, we perceive your divinity, which strengthens our faith; we glimpse your resurrected glory, which strengthens our hope; and we are invited into an experience of profound intimacy, which strengthens our love.

So often our life gets weighed down by our own way of seeing things and with negative ideas. Thank you for the incomparable beauty of your Transfiguration, which changes the way we look at everything. What we see in you, you want to impart to us. May the grace of your Transfiguration increase our expectation, and move us to keep our attention fixed on you. Obedient to the Father, may we always listen to you. With trust in the newness you radiate in the Transfiguration, I offer you my intentions: (mention your request here).

August 15

The Assumption of the Blessed Virgin Mary

THE MYSTERY of the Assumption of the Blessed Virgin Mary proclaims to the world that there is a heaven, and that heaven is our destiny. The miracle of the Assumption testifies to the exceptionality of Mary's supreme holiness. So surpassing is the blessedness of the Blessed Virgin Mary that God summons the whole of her — body and soul — to heaven, and that fact is revealed to the world as an article of faith.

This makes sense logically. St. Thomas Aquinas points out that the last curse common to fallen men and women is that they must return to dust. Mary, however, never tainted by original sin, remained free from this curse.[7] Hence, the most appropriate response to Mary's dormition, or "falling asleep," was her bodily "translation" to heaven, and not that of committing her body to the earth. With Our Lady's arrival, heaven at last becomes complete. Until Mary joined the company of the angels and the elect, something vital remained missing. There was a vacant seat next to the resurrected Christ awaiting the presence of the assumed Mother of God. And just as once the Blessed Virgin clothed the eternal Word with flesh at the Annunciation, the eternal Word clothes Mary with his own power and mercy at the Assumption (St. Bernard).[8]

Moreover, Mary's assumption endows her with an ability impossible on earth. The physical constraints of worldly existence precluded

Our Lady's reach to anyone beyond the limited geographical area in which she lived. But now from heaven, the Mother of God can see, know, and love us all with the same maternal love with which she embraced those privileged to walk with her on earth. Mary's new closeness with God promises *us* a new closeness with God otherwise inconceivable.

And finally, Mary assumed into heaven "has left behind clear footprints for those coming after" (St. Amadeus of Lausanne).[9] The Assumption of the Blessed Virgin Mary is the promise of our own future bodily resurrection. Blessed John Paul II assures us that our "hope is enriched with ever new reasons," for Mary in the Assumption communicates to us "an ever new capacity to await God's future."[10]

Novena Prayer

O Blessed Virgin Mary, your glorious assumption into heaven is a promise of our future destiny. You are the beginning and image of the Church's coming to perfection. Now your maternal love knows no earthly limits or constraints. From your place in heaven, your love reaches each one of us on earth. And just as you are physically exalted to the heavens, so too your motherly intercession assumes its zenith.

Your new closeness with God in paradise bestows upon us a new closeness with God. Your assumption enriches our hope with ever-new reasons. The glory of this mystery blesses us with the graced capacity to await the future that God has in store for us. May the glory of your holy assumption move me to abandon myself to the Lord's promises. Our Lady assumed into heaven, with thankfulness and joy I confide to you my intentions: (mention your request here).

August 22

THE QUEENSHIP OF THE BLESSED VIRGIN MARY

THE BOOK OF REVELATION gives us a glimpse of the Queen of heaven: "A great sign appeared in heaven, a woman clothed with the sun, … and on her head a crown of twelve stars" (Rev 12:1). The liturgical memorial of the Queenship of the Blessed Virgin Mary — along with her coronation commemorated as a mystery of the Rosary — reveals one more dimension of God's mercy toward us. Sin darkens our intellect, weakens our will, and leaves us prey to enticements contrary to reason. We are tempted to despair over our powerlessness and our inclination toward evil. God gives us Mary, the Queen of heaven, to assure us that we are not dominated by our feelings, our limitations, or our passions. The Blessed Mother is Queen over all these things.

God has so designed his divine providence that the Mother of God is not separated from the Son of God's dominion and power. St. Anthony of Padua (d. 1231) observes that inasmuch as God the Father and the Blessed Virgin Mary had the same Son, Mary merited to be crowned Queen in heaven.[11] Mary as Queen, says Blessed John Paul II, participates deeply in the life and love of the risen Christ, giving to others all she possesses, and dedicating herself to the work of salvation.[12] "Seeing that we are unworthy to receive God's graces immediately from his hand," explains St. Bernard (d. 1153), "God gives them to Mary, in order that through her we may receive all that he wishes to give us."[13] Through the Blessed Virgin Mary, Jesus reigns over the world (St. Louis de Montfort).[14]

As Queen, Mary keeps us close to Christ and takes the matter of our salvation into her own charge. St. Thomas Aquinas tells us that since the Blessed Virgin Mary has been entrusted with the keys and treasures of heaven, through Mary's intercession many souls are in paradise who would otherwise not be there had she not interceded for them.[15] Blessed Henry Suso (d. 1366) counsels us: "When our heart is oppressed with grief and fear and can find no remedy for its suffering, we have no recourse but to look upward to the Queen of Heaven."[16]

Novena Prayer

Blessed Virgin Mary, Queen of heaven and earth, you participate deeply in the life and love of your risen Son. You exercise your Queenship by cooperating in the work of the redemption of the human race. United with Jesus, you share in the diffusion of God's grace in the world. You give to those who implore you all that you possess.

Whenever my emotions, my understanding, or my will threaten to dominate my life, come close to me with your sovereign love. Your glorious state enables you to follow us in our daily earthly journey. When our hearts are oppressed with grief and fear, and we can find no remedy, let us have recourse to you. Holy Queen enthroned above, you are our life, our sweetness, and our hope. I look with trust to you, Blessed Virgin Mary, my Queen, as I confide my intentions: (mention your request here).

SEPTEMBER

September 8

THE NATIVITY OF THE
BLESSED VIRGIN MARY

AT THE BIRTH of the Blessed Virgin Mary, the
Immaculate Conception is made visible for all to
see. Today we can begin to carry out Jesus' dying
desire: "Behold, your mother!" (Jn 19:27). As we
gaze upon the beauty of Mary, we experience the
reversal of the evil effects of the fall of both angels and humankind. St. Bonaventure (d. 1274)
explains that the devil, created good by God, was
destined to be perfected by the movement of his
affection toward the highest good — God. But
the sight of his own beauty and eminence made
him fall in love with himself. Thus the angel fell,
perverting everything to indulge his pride and
his own private good.[1]

However, when Mary looks upon her own
beauty manifested at her nativity, the sight moves
the affection of her Immaculate Heart to the Highest Good — and she takes us with her. The saints
tell us that the Blessed Virgin was born from the
long-barren womb of her mother, Anne, in order
to prefigure the deliverance which was to come
to us through Mary from the curse incurred by
Adam and Eve.[2] In particular, with the unveiling

of Mary's face at her birth, we are given a sign
of God's mercy and tenderness for us. Mary is a
"living icon of the Father's mercy" (Blessed John
Paul II)[3] — a joy for us *before* Jesus is born, and
a consolation for Christ's heavy-hearted disciples
after Jesus ascends into heaven.

The image of God lost in Eden is retrieved in
the birth of Mary (Johannes Tauler).[4] Even more,
says Bishop Bossuet, in the nativity of Mary God
gives us an "outline" of Jesus Christ — a creature
who "is in some sort a living expression of Jesus'
own perfections."[5] The Byzantine Liturgy hails the
birth of Mary for revealing to the world a "living
heaven": through the nativity of the Mother of
God "the earth is united to heaven for the salvation of our souls. Today is the end of the barrenness of our nature."[6] St. Gregory Palamas (d. 1359)
exclaims, "Today a new world and a mysterious
paradise have been revealed."[7] At Mary's nativity,
we return to the origin of countless blessings.

Novena Prayer

*Blessed Virgin Mary, with untellable joy we cel-
ebrate your nativity. For by it, a new world and
a mysterious paradise are revealed to all God's
people. We are led away from our condition of
slavery, just as darkness yields before the coming*

of the light. Our hearts overflow with thankfulness to God for the gift of your life, given to destroy the kingdom of sorrow.

Your birth is the end of our death. Your birthday fills the world with a sweet consolation and a holy joy, for from you comes Jesus, who will save us from our sins. It is a day of exultation, for the barrenness of our nature has come to an end. When we look at you, Mary, we see that the hand of the Holy Spirit has written the Trinity in you. Blessed Virgin, with devotion I offer you my intentions: (mention your request here).

September 12

THE MOST HOLY NAME OF MARY

THIS FEAST REVEALS God's "Marian devotion." For when we pray the Ave Maria, we echo the divine encounter with the Blessed Virgin at the Annunciation. However, while we say, "Hail, Mary," what the angel actually utters is, "Hail, favored one!" (Lk 1:28, NABRE). Which suggests that the name "Mary" and "Favored One" are meant to be considered interchangeable. When we say Mary's holy name, we share in the fullness of grace that the Mother of God is.

St. Peter Canisius (d. 1597), doctor of the Church, makes the claim that, after the Holy Name of Jesus, there is no other name more glorious or powerful than the holy name of Mary.[8] Or, as Blessed Henry Suso puts it, "O Mary, what must you yourself be, since your very name is so loving and gracious?"[9] And since heaven is the first ever to pray the Hail Mary — when the angelic messenger communicated the intention of God himself — that invocation retains a permanent, incomparable role in the economy of salvation. In fact, praying the Hail Mary, instructs St. Louis de Montfort, will "cause the Word of God to take root in the soul and bring forth Jesus, the Fruit of Life" just as it did in the womb of the Blessed Virgin.[10]

The very ability to pronounce the name of Mary with faith and love is a verification of blessedness. As St. Louis de Montfort explains: "Those who show positive signs of being among the elect appreciate and love the Hail Mary, and are always glad to say it…. The frequent thought and loving invocation of Mary is a sure indication that the soul is not estranged from God by sin."[11]

And as much as Mary's holy name is a blessing for us, it is a dread for the evil one. Venerable Thomas à Kempis (d. 1471) observes that the devils fear Mary so much that, if they but hear her holy name pronounced, they fly from the person who speaks it as if from a burning fire.[12] For this reason, we devoutly follow the indispensable counsel of St. Bernard: "In dangers, in straits, in perplexity, call upon Mary. Let her name be always in your mouth and in your heart."[13]

NOVENA PRAYER

Hail, Mary, Highly Favored One. Everything changed when an archangel spoke your name. Your glorious name is a blessing from heaven that draws the divine close and causes devils to flee. Through my devout invocation of your holy name, may the Word of God take root in my soul and bring forth Jesus, the Fruit of Life. May the power of your holy name pierce through all my shame, all my lukewarmness, and all my self-loathing. In the gift of your holy name, you make yourself accessible to us, desiring to be intimately known.

May your holy name be always in my mouth and in my heart. The frequent thought and loving utterance of your holy name assures me that my soul is not estranged from God by sin. Holy Mary, with full confidence in the power of your holy name, I offer you my intentions: (mention your request here).

September 14

THE EXALTATION OF THE HOLY CROSS

THE CROSS is a gift of God the Father to his Son, by which Jesus demonstrates his obedience to his Father and proves the depths of his love for us. We exalt the holy cross by embracing its God-given purpose. St. John Chrysostom (d. 407) calls the cross the Father's will, "a sword against sin."[14] The cross separates us from whatever separates us from God. St. Peter testifies that Jesus himself "bore our sins in his body on the tree, that we might die to sin and live to righteousness" (1 Pt 2:24).

We need this instrument of purification to save us from the trap of self-sufficiency. Out of love, our Savior repeatedly commands: "If any man would come after me, let him deny himself and take up his cross and follow me.... He who does not take his cross and follow me is not worthy of me" (Mt 16:24; 10:38). The suffering of the cross is calculated to destroy in us any secret attachments we rely on. "I believe that the cross will not be satisfied," wrote Paul Claudel (d. 1955), "until that point when it has destroyed in you everything that is not the will of God."[15] St. Paul gives eloquent witness to this mystery:

I have been crucified with Christ; it is no longer I who live, but Christ.... Far be it from me to glory except in the cross of our Lord Jesus Christ, by which the world has been crucified to me.... Those who belong to Christ Jesus have crucified the flesh with its passions and desires. (Gal 2:20; 6:14; 5:24)

Father Simon Tugwell observes that

It is the cross and only the cross that provides a constant point of reference in the chaos of our world, because *there* is all our poverty and helplessness and pain, all our yearning and all our mutual injustice, taken up into the stillness of God's everlasting love and made into the instrument and revelation of his unchanging will.[16]

To live the triumph of the cross is to "glorify God by allowing ourselves to be drawn into the act of love that was accomplished on the cross" (Massimo Camisasca).[17]

Novena Prayer

Loving Savior, your holy cross is a gift from the Father to save us from our sins. We exalt the holy

*cross by allowing ourselves to be drawn into the
radical act of love you accomplished on the cross.
Give me the grace to take up my cross daily and
follow you in faith, for the mercy of your cross
destroys in me the secret attachments that would
separate me from you. The triumph on the cross
appears by transforming all my failings, imperfection, impossibility, fear, doubt, and evil. God's suc-
cess comes about through the cross and is always
found under that sign.*

*Let me sign myself often with the cross so as to
place myself under its singular protection. By the
power of the holy cross, make my life one of total
self-surrender to you. Glorying in your holy cross,
I offer you my intentions: (mention your request
here).*

September 15

OUR LADY OF SORROWS

THE CRUCIFIED JESUS commands his mother,
"Behold, your son!" (Jn 19:26). He means every
one of us. Behold us where? In the midst of our
own daily crucifixions. Behold us how? Blessed
John Paul II says that "Mary's sharing in the
drama of the cross makes this event more deeply

human and helps the faithful to enter into the mystery…. Mary's hope at the foot of the cross contains a light stronger than the darkness that reigns in many hearts."[18] The presence of Mary at Calvary inserts the full force of her immaculate, glorious humanity into an act of horrific inhumanity. The curse of loneliness lies at the root of all human misery and wretchedness, but that misery is worsened when we are alone in our suffering. God wants us never to be alone again when we experience the cross; the mystery of Our Lady of Sorrows is the way out of alienation, desolation, and despair.

St. Albert the Great (d. 1280) observes that if all the world is under obligation to Jesus for his Passion, then all the world is under obligation to Our Lady of Sorrows for her compassion.[19] The meaning of suffering stands as one of the most trying mysteries of human existence. The fullest source of the answer to that question can only be found in love — it is given to us by God in flesh: in the crucified Christ and in his attending, sorrowful mother. St. Leo the Great states that Mary not only deserves to be called merciful, but even mercy itself.[20]

"The divine Redeemer," writes Pope John Paul II, "wishes to penetrate the soul of every sufferer through the heart of his holy Mother."[21] It is a heart we can trust because it, too, has been

pierced. Blessed Henry Suso prays, "My wounds
are known to you, loving Mother.... When I completely despair of God and of myself, thinking of
you, recalling you, my spirit comes alive again as
if out of the deepest darkness."[22] No wonder the
Mother of God stands by the cross of her Son, for
suffering itself is a kind of mother: "Suffering is
present in the world ... in order to give birth to
works of love towards neighbor."[23]

NOVENA PRAYER

*Our Lady of Sorrows, your presence at the cross of
your Son transformed the horror of that event and
made it more deeply human. Our devout union
with you, Sorrowful Mother, enables us to enter
into that mystery — for the hope you radiate at
the foot of the cross contains a light greater than all
the world's darkness. Bless me with that hope, for
so often the darkness threatens to overwhelm me.*

*Through your Immaculate Heart, our Redeem-
er wishes to penetrate the soul of everyone who suf-
fers. You stand at the cross of Jesus Christ so that,
when I experience the crucifixion in my own life,
I will know that I am not alone in my anguish —
you, Mother of Compassion, are there with me, offering me your love. With confidence in your maternal mediation to turn every evil from me, I offer
you my intentions: (mention your request here).*

September 29

STS. MICHAEL, GABRIEL, AND RAPHAEL, ARCHANGELS

THE IMPORTANCE OF THE ANGELS in our life can be gauged by their prevalence in Christ's. Angels appear at Christ's conception, at his birth, in his temptations in the desert, in his parables and teaching, in the garden during his agony, at his tomb, and at his ascension. The *Catechism of the Catholic Church* teaches that "the whole life of the Church benefits from the mysterious and powerful help of angels" (CCC 334, cf. Acts 5:18-20; 8:26-29; 10:3-8; 12:6-11; Job 33:23-24; Zech 1:12; Tob 12:12).

But why do we need angels? St. Hilary of Poitiers (d. 368) tells us that it is the weakness of human beings which warrants their service. Angels are sent for the sake of those who will inherit salvation. "In our weakness we are impoverished for a minister of spiritual intercession [to act on our behalf] in the matter of beseeching and propitiating."[24]

Angels make human beings' "alienation and perishableness more endurable, showing them in various ways that they are not abandoned, but rather that God is forging new links with them" (Adrienne von Speyr).[25] In fact, "some have entertained angels unawares" (Heb 13:2). *The Golden Legend* explains that angels intervene upon seeing our need of their aid since, after all, there are bad angels at work, warring against us. The good angels are sent to inflame our hearts with love, to enlighten our understanding and bring us to knowledge, and to strengthen any weakness in us. Even more, the angels bear our souls up to heaven in three ways: by preparing the way, by conveying the souls to heaven along the prepared way, and by putting the souls in their place in heaven.[26]

The Gospel reveals that "there is joy before the angels of God over one sinner who repents" (Lk 15:10). The second-century Christian text *The Shepherd of Hermas* counsels, "The angel of righteousness is gentle and modest, meek and peaceful. When he ascends into your heart, he talks to you of righteousness, purity, chastity, contentment, and of every righteous deed and glorious virtue. Trust him and his works."[27] Through our honoring of the holy angels, may what was said of St. Stephen at his martyrdom be spoken also of us: "His face was like the face of an angel" (Acts 6:15).

Novena Prayer

Blessed Archangels, you exist to give glory to God. In the Mass, we ask to join you in singing your hymn of glory to the Father, for we long to form with you one chorus of exultant praise. Thank you for your friendship.

Archangel Michael, whose name means "who is like God," you never cease to fight the enemies of heaven, rescuing us from our fears. Archangel Raphael, whose name means "God has healed," through your companionship we have been healed. Archangel Gabriel, whose name means "God is my strength," you were the messenger of the Annunciation to the Blessed Virgin Mary. May we, like her, always be surrendered to the Word of life that you bear.

Pray that our lives may be like yours in the angelic way we seek to care for others. Accompany us always, especially in offering to God these, my intentions: (mention your request here).

OCTOBER

October 2

THE HOLY GUARDIAN ANGELS

THE GUARDIAN ANGELS are a proof of how much God loves us. He sends the guardian angels to protect and attend us, especially when we do not know how to take care of ourselves. St. Basil the Great teaches that "beside each believer stands an angel as protector and shepherd leading him to life" (CCC 336; St. Basil, *Adv. Eunomium* III, 1: PG 29, 656B). This prompts St. Jerome (d. 420) to comment, "How great the dignity of the soul, since each one has from his birth an angel commissioned to guard it."[1]

We need our angelic protectors, explains St. Thomas Aquinas, because, although we can to a certain degree avoid evil thanks to free will, we cannot do so in any sufficient degree. Just as guardians are appointed for people who have to pass by an unsafe road, so an angel guardian is assigned to each human being as long as that one is a wayfarer. Guardian angels regulate us and move us to good by instructing us, by assisting us in prayer, by warding off demons, and by preventing both bodily and spiritual harm.[2]

St. Gregory of Nyssa (d. 395) tells us that "the Lord of the angels procures life and peace through his angels for those who are worthy."[3] And St. Ignatius (first century) adds, "It is characteristic of God and his angels that in their activity they give true joy and spiritual exultation, while removing the sadness and affliction that the enemy excites."[4] Father Simon Tugwell, O.P., describes the distinctive help offered by the angels:

> They cannot give us the warm, animal, emotional kind of support that we get from other human beings, but the very simplicity of their spiritual vision can help to alleviate the complexity of our animal life. The purity of their praise can come to our assistance when we are bogged down in the turmoil of our sensuality or our emotions and can find no way through. When we are weighed down by our corruptible flesh, we can be lifted up, like our Lord in Gethsemane, by the spiritual joy of the angels.[5]

St. Edith Stein assures us, "It is their bliss to be allowed to cooperate in God's dispensing of graces."[6]

Novena Prayer

My good Guardian Angel, you have been appointed by God to be my protector and shepherd, leading me to life and peace. Thank you for your guardianship. Without the benefit of your angelic care, I would be left to the custody of my own feeble resources. You delight in dispensing God's graces to aid me in my salvation.

Regulate my life and move me to the good. Instruct me that I may live by the enlightenment of heaven. Assist me in prayer. Ward off demons that would threaten me, and remove the sadness and affliction brought on by the enemy. When weighed down by my emotions and fleshly things, lift me up and let me share your joy. Protect me from all bodily and spiritual harm.

Please forgive any times I may have neglected you. With trust in your angelic protection, I offer you my intentions: (mention your request here).

October 7

OUR LADY OF THE ROSARY

WE BECOME CHRISTIAN not through lofty ideas or ethical choices, but through an encounter with the person of Jesus Christ and his saving events. The more we return to those events in meditation and self-surrender, the more we grow in holiness. If we are humble, we recognize our inability to do this worthily and well, for sin clouds our reason and weakens our will. We need a blessed companion — Our Lady — who enables us to rise above our faults and limitations so as to penetrate the mysteries of the Gospel. God gives us all this in the Rosary.

The Rosary is a way we continue to live out the graces we receive in the liturgy since it contains all the depth of the Gospel in its entirety. The Rosary opens us to the depths of the heart of Christ so that we can enter into his heart more profoundly. The design of the Rosary, with its cycles of meditation, awakens in us an always-increasing thirst for a deeper inner knowledge of the mystery of Christ.

While serving as a unique and most effective means of fostering contemplation, the Rosary also sheds light on the mystery of being human, for the mysteries of the Rosary mark the rhythm of human life. God communicates himself to us according to those rhythms. The Rosary thereby shapes our existence and conforms us ever more closely to Christ through a kind of training in holiness by which we are changed into his likeness. And since no one has ever been as devoted to the contemplation of the face of Christ as faithfully as Mary, Our Lady plays an indispensable role in our meditation of the Rosary.

The Mother of God constantly sets before us the mysteries of her Son with the desire that our devout contemplation of those mysteries will release all their saving power. Mary acts to train us and to mold us, making us sensitive and alert to Jesus — able to "read" him — until Christ is fully formed in our Christian life. United with Our Lady of the Rosary, we encounter the beauty of Christ's face and experience the profoundness of his love.

Novena Prayer

Our Lady of the Rosary, I long to grow in my understanding of what it means to be human so that I can devote my humanity to living for God. The blessing of the Rosary helps to shape our existence and conform us more closely to Christ, for it contains all the depth of the Gospel. You constantly set before us the mysteries of your Son so that, contemplating those mysteries united with you, their saving power will take effect in our lives. Help me to reflect upon the mysteries of the heart of Christ and to integrate them into my life.

May the Rosary awaken in me an always-increasing thirst for a deeper inner knowledge of the mystery of Christ. Help me to be changed into God's likeness through my praying of the Rosary.

With confidence in your maternal mediation, I offer you my intentions: (mention your request here).

October

WORLD MISSION DAY

MISSION SUNDAY is celebrated on the next-to-last Sunday in October. The risen Jesus delivers his missionary mandate: "Go therefore and make disciples of all nations, baptizing them in the name of the Father and of the Son and of the Holy Spirit" (Mt 28:19). Jesus always identified his "I" with his mission: loving obedience to the Father, committed to reconciling the alienated world to God, even at the expense of his own life. "The missionary thrust," says Blessed John Paul II, "belongs to the very nature of the Christian life." Missionary activity has but one purpose: "to serve man by revealing to him the love of God made manifest in Jesus Christ."[7]

Gospel missionaries share a conviction: to be human is to be filled with the expectation of knowing the truth about God and about humanity. Faith must be offered to the multitudes because they have the right to know the riches of the mystery of Christ and to share in the radical newness of life he brings. The authentic Christian proposal of faith is always an appeal to reason and an orientation toward the Truth itself.

Perhaps the most compelling reason for us to be missionaries is that, at one point in time, someone was a missionary of God's love and mercy to us. "Mission is possible only as the echo of a lived fraternal friendship, because it is the echo of a forgiveness that has been received" (Massimo Camisasca).[8] The change that took place in us as a result of that encounter with Jesus Christ remains the most attractive thing about us. This is why Pope John Paul II says that mission means "communicating to others the reasons for your own conversion."[9] "Mission consists in recalling people's hearts from inside their situation to something that is happening among them just as it happened among us" (Massimo Camisasca).[10]

The essence of mission is to attract others to enter into the intimacy of the Church. The willingness to engage in mission is an accurate indicator of our faith in Christ and his love for us. And faith cannot help but be strengthened when it is given to others.

Novena Prayer

Loving Father, to be Christian is to share in the life of God who seeks at every moment to communicate his very self in love. In this way, the Christian life is missionary. Thank you for the witnesses to the Gospel you sent into my life who led me to communion with you. Help me to be an effective missionary and to draw many people into faith-filled friendship with you. Let me communicate to others the reasons for my conversion. May they see in my life of faith an echo of the forgiveness I received. Enable me to overcome any fear or reluctance I have to witness to Jesus Christ.

Bless and protect all foreign missionaries. May the truth of the Gospel be proclaimed to all nations and peoples who do not yet believe in Jesus Christ. United in your Son, I offer you my intentions: (mention your request here).

NOVEMBER

November 1

ALL SAINTS

"THE SAINT IS A PERSON who is so fascinated by the beauty of God and by his perfect truth as to be progressively transformed by it" (Pope Benedict XVI).[1] Sanctity comes about through a person's self-surrendering dependence on God and his holy will. The glory of the saint consists in the communion that he or she shares with God and all the blessed. We honor "so great a cloud of witnesses" (Heb 12:1) by renewing our desire to join them.

St. Thérèse of Lisieux (d. 1897) promised before she died that she would spend her heaven doing good on earth. In fact, helping us who still labor to get to heaven stands out as one of the chief joys of the saints. "The holy ones on earth become endless bliss to all who are in heaven" (Blessed Julian of Norwich).[2] The saints intercede on our behalf, beseeching God to grant our petitions a gracious hearing. To this they add a second form of intervention: applying the good works and merits of their own holy lives to our petitions, "even as the shedding of Christ's blood is said to ask pardon for us" (St. Thomas Aquinas).[3]

Additionally, God allots certain special graces to his saints, and he entrusts them with the responsibility of administering and distributing these graces. Having and praying to our patron saints, or to saints renowned for particular causes, relieves the tediousness that sometimes arises in prayer, and causes the fervor of our devotion to grow. Through this wonderful " 'abundant exchange of all good things' (*Indulgentiarum Doctrina*, 5) … the holiness of one profits others" (CCC 1475). As we rely on the saints in humility and gratitude, the friendship forged with the elect draws us into the very intimacy they share with God.

True models of holiness and exemplars of grace, "the saints have always been the source and origin of renewal in the most difficult moments in the Church's history" (CCC 828; John Paul II, *CL* 16, 3). They are our hope, our unfailing encouragement, our edification, and our promise of a predestined happiness — for when we look at the saints, we know that holiness is real, and that the sanctity they now live forever we can live too … with their help.

NOVENA PRAYER

Merciful Father, one outstanding proof of your love for us is that you give us friends to accompany us in the life of faith — the saints. The blessed com-

munion the saints share with you in heaven is the longed-for desire of our heart. The saints are our friends in faith, our models of hope, our exemplars of holiness, our companions in suffering, our mediators in need, our heroes in taking up the cross. Out of love for us, the saints apply the merits of their holy lives to our poor prayers, and so aid us in our salvation. Thank you for my patron saints. Help me to depend on them with great confidence.

I long to be a saint. Please convert my life and configure it to the life of your beloved Son. Calling upon the intercession of my patron saints, I offer you my intentions: (mention your request here).

November 2

THE COMMEMORATION OF ALL THE FAITHFUL DEPARTED (ALL SOULS' DAY)

THE CHURCH TEACHES that truly penitent people who die in God's grace and friendship before they have made the necessary satisfaction for their sins experience the cleansing of their souls by purgatorial sufferings after death. "Every sin … entails an unhealthy attachment to creatures, which must be purified either here on earth, or after death in the state called Purgatory" (CCC

1472). The suffrages of the living — prayers, sacrifices, works of penance, indulgences — profit the Holy Souls for the relief of their sufferings, helping to gain for them the holiness necessary to enter the joy of heaven.

Pope Benedict XVI holds that if there were no purgatory, then hope would move us to invent it. "Purgatory basically means that God can put the pieces back together again," and we could not live without the possibility of such mercy.[4] Purgatory is an inward process of transformation by which a still imperfectly purified soul becomes capable of Christ and the communion of saints. In purgatory, says St. Claude de la Colombière, we are certain never to oppose the will of God, never to resent his severity; we shall even love the rigors of his justice, and wait with patience until it becomes entirely appeased.[5]

In her famous treatise on purgatory, St. Catherine of Genoa (d. 1510) says that the pain which the holy souls endure because of what they have willfully done to displease God "is greater than other pain they feel."[6] At the same time,

a great happiness is granted [to the holy souls] that grows ... as they draw nearer [to] God.... For every glimpse which can be had of God exceeds any pain or joy [a person] can feel. [The holy souls] clearly see God to be on fire with extreme and pure love for them. Strongly and unceasingly this love draws the soul with that uniting look, as though it had nought else than this to do.[7]

It cannot be doubted, says St. Augustine, that the prayers of the Church for the holy souls move God to treat them with more clemency than their sins deserve. What a great joy and consolation to know that our love can reach into the afterlife.

NOVENA PRAYER

Merciful Father, you regard the holy souls in purgatory with a special, tender love. They died in your grace and friendship, but imperfectly purified. Now they undergo the purification needed to enter the joy of heaven in radiant holiness. Thank you for this most excellent work of mercy by which you allow us to help our neighbors beyond the grave. As the holy souls draw nearer to you, you grant them a great happiness.

By my sacrifices, almsgiving, and prayers for the dead, may the holy souls clearly see how you are on fire with extreme love for them. May the prayers of the Church relieve the holy souls and move you to

treat them with more clemency than their sins de-
serve. Let me be mindful of the holy souls and love
them in true friendship. United with their power-
ful prayers, I offer you my intentions: (mention
your request here).

November 9

THE DEDICATION OF THE LATERAN BASILICA

TODAY'S FEAST COMMEMORATES the anniversary
of the dedication of the Lateran Basilica, which is
the cathedral church of Rome. It is this basilica
(and not St. Peter's Basilica) that holds the dis-
tinction of being the episcopal seat of the pope
as bishop of Rome. The Lateran (named for the
family that donated the land on which the church
stands) served as the residence of the popes for
about a thousand years, beginning in the fourth
century, and hosted five ecumenical councils.

Even more, this historic church holds particular significance for Catholics everywhere because
it is honored, as the inscription over the entrance
of the basilica declares, as "the mother and head
of all churches in the Holy City and throughout
the World." Catholicism's mother church reminds

us that the Church *is* a Mother. God willed to save and sanctify us by making us his people through the Mother of our new birth, the Church. That happened, both physically and mystically, when we came into the Church at our baptism.

The special reverence we pay today to the Lateran Basilica spills over to all Catholic churches, for they remain the geographical locus where the Mystery continues to draw close to us. As Christ's disciples witnessed Jesus cleansing the Temple, they were struck by a line from Psalm 69: "Zeal for your house has consumed me" (v. 9). And that same zeal consumes us because, like the Jerusalem Temple, every church is a "privileged place of encounter with God" (CCC 584). What distinguishes the pilgrim from a tourist who enters a church building is motivation — a pilgrim goes in as if going home. The believer is edified by the church edifice inasmuch as it directs the Christian's mind and heart to our ultimate home in heaven.

The concrete, crossable threshold of a church symbolizes how much we need to pass from a "world wounded by sin to the world of the new Life" (CCC 1186). The very sight of a church building signals that a Christian community lives nearby and will gather in the sacred place to worship God, to grow in its religion, and to delight in the belonging of faith. It generates hope!

Novena Prayer

Loving Father, you created the world for the sake of communion with your divine life — a communion brought about through a convocation called the Church. You willed to save and sanctify us by making us your people through the Church, our Mother. The heavenly Jerusalem is foreshadowed in visible church buildings. How many times have I found consolation by stepping into a church and praying before the tabernacle of your Son? How often have I received assurance from seeing a house of God that reminds me of my true home with you?

The whole People of God is on pilgrimage to our true heavenly home. As a faithful member of the Body of Christ, may I, by the witness of my life, make visible to others the presence of Christ's Church in the world. United with your Son, the Head of the Church, I offer you my intentions: (mention your request here).

November 21

The Presentation of the Blessed Virgin Mary

As we celebrate the feast of the Presentation of the Blessed Virgin Mary in the Temple, our minds travel to the presentation of Jesus in that same Temple, which will follow in not so many years. The fact that this mystery marks the life of both mother and son bears significance for us. The child Mary and the infant Jesus are taken to the Temple — the privileged place of encounter with God. Their identity is revealed in their closeness to the Father, symbolized by the presentation. Mary and Jesus are borne to the Temple so that we may share in their closeness with God. As Blessed John Paul II notes, "The whole of the universe is in some way touched by the divine favor with which the Father looks upon Mary."[8]

According to tradition, Our Lady's parents, Joachim and Anne, accompany their little girl to the Temple so that, there, they might both fulfill a vow they have made to God and also obtain an education for their daughter. On the part of Mary, it is an early occasion to demonstrate her total dedication to God's service and her utter obedience to God's will. The Byzantine Liturgy lauds Mary:

> O Virgin Mother of God, you ... are the pride of the martyrs and the cause of the renewal of the entire human race, for through you we have been reconciled with God. Wherefore we honor your entrance into the Temple of the Lord, ... for we are saved

through your intercession, O most honor-
able one![9]

The saints compare Mary, in her presentation in the Temple, to the dove of Noah's ark that
brought the captives of the great flood the promise of new life in an olive branch. Mary brings us
the good news of the birth of salvation — a birth
that will come, not through the twig of a tree, but
through the wood of the cross. Commenting on
Mary's presentation, St. Gregory of Palamas (d.
1359) writes,

> The all-pure Virgin made her departure
> from mankind when she entered the Holy
> of Holies; then she went back among men
> in order that, being pre-eminent in holi-
> ness, she might share the inalienable gift
> of hallowing with everyone. Nowhere was
> excluded, not even the world's secret place,
> that innermost sanctuary.[10]

Novena Prayer

*Most Blessed Mother, as you are presented in the
Temple, you are drawn more deeply into the Father's embrace of love. This offering of yourself is
a demonstration of your total dedication to God's*

service and of your perfect obedience to his will. Let me share in your offering of self. Take my offering into your maternal hands. Purify and complete it so that it may be agreeable to God. The whole of the universe is touched by the divine favor with which the Father looks upon you.

By your prayer and holy example, help me re-dedicate myself to serving God in every aspect of my life, and to being completely abandoned to his divine will. By your blessed presentation in the Temple, you bring us the promise of reconciliation with God and the hope of new life. Entrusting myself to your powerful maternal intercession, I offer my intentions: (mention your request here).

November

OUR LORD JESUS CHRIST, KING OF THE UNIVERSE

WE VOICE OUR LONGING for Christ to be our King every time we pray the Our Father, pleading, "Thy kingdom come!" What kind of King is Christ? When Pontius Pilate questions Jesus about his kingship (see Jn 18:33-37), the Son of God declares that he is born to testify to the truth: the truth that purifies us of self-centeredness; the truth that prevents us from reducing the meaning of life to the things we can do; the truth that gives us the courage to be humble and that leads us to our true selves.

Christ the King is the Truth who sets us free. We see this played out dramatically on Calvary. The Good Thief, gazing at the crucified Christ, finds in the Savior what he had but grasped at in his life of crime. Christ, enthroned on the cross, moves the Good Thief to beg, "Jesus, remember me when you come into your kingdom" (Lk 23:42, NABRE). Our Lord reveals his startling majesty in the promise of mercy. Jesus will not desert his cross when taunters deride him, because a true king always seeks the common good of his people over against his own private profit. Christ's kingship is a reign of love that vanquishes every tyranny of our life.

Our response is adoration: "homage of the spirit to the 'King of Glory' (Ps 24:9-10)" that "exalts the greatness of the Lord" (CCC 2628). Christ the King communicates to us "the gift of royal freedom" by which, as St. Ambrose says, we exercise "a kind of royal power" over our person, refusing to let "passions breed rebellion" within, and not permitting ourselves to be "imprisoned by sin" (CCC 908; St. Ambrose, *Psal.* 118:14:30: PL 15:1476).

St. Gregory of Nyssa tells us that "the soul shows its royal ... character" — its likeness to the King — "in that it is free and self-governed" (*Veritatis Splendor*, 38). Christ enters into his kingship by acting like a servant toward us. Christ the King returns at the Second Coming seated "on his glorious throne" (Mt 25:31), rewarding those who imitate the compassionate, kingly service he bestows upon those most in need (see Mt 25:34-40).

Novena Prayer

Lord Jesus Christ our King, your kingship is a rule of love that seeks and finds us in ways that are always new. I love and worship you as the Lord and Master of my life. Be the King of my heart, my soul, my mind, and my strength. Reign over my weakness, my problems, my worries, my hurts, my fears, my longings, my imperfections, and my trials. When my feelings, ideas, passions, or emotions threaten to dominate my life, come swiftly with your sovereign power.

Your kingship is a reign of love vanquishing every tyranny of our life. Bless my life with your gift of royal freedom. May I constantly turn my life over to you in homage of spirit exalting your greatness as Lord. Make my life one of perpetual obedi-

ence and adoration. With longing for the coming of God's kingdom, I offer my intentions: (mention your request here).

November

FIRST SUNDAY OF ADVENT

THE LONGING THAT CONSUMED the hearts of the ancient Jewish people finds a voice in Psalm 42: "My soul thirsts for God, for the living God. When shall I come and behold the face of God?" (v. 2). This conveys their urgent anticipation of a Messiah who would come to save them from persecution, oppression, and all that afflicted and disabled them. Advent is a kind of mini-sharing in that expectation.

Since our heart is made for God, it remains restless until it is one with him. To be myself, I need Someone Else. Yet not only do we at times forget God in our daily life, we also disregard the gnawing of our heart and attempt to fill it with what cannot satisfy. This leads to frustration, addiction, and depression. What can rescue us from such alienation from our very selves? We need God as close to us as flesh and blood — we ache to see his face. That is why each year, through the

grace of Advent, God blesses us with a new beginning — a chance to start again and hand ourselves over to what really matters.

In the season of Advent, the Lord woos us with
words that will become Christ's first in the Gospel of John: "What are you looking for?" (Jn 1:38,
NABRE). Advent is the arrival of the beginning
of a Presence — a Presence that moves us to say
"Yes," with the Blessed Virgin Mary, to what we
are really waiting for in life. Even as God comes
to us, he calls us to go out to meet him, like the
shepherds and the Magi. This is a call to conversion — to leave behind whatever keeps us closed
in on ourselves. Filled with the certainty and joy
that Christ's closeness brings, we ask God in the
opening prayer of the First Sunday of Advent for
"the resolve to run forth to meet your Christ."
Our happiness consists in abandoning ourselves
to his power.

We beg that God's grace, like a good friend, will
always go before us and follow after us. We want to
live our Advent loving the people we meet with the
same love we hope to receive on Christmas.

Novena Prayer

Come, Lord Jesus. Come, you who are Wisdom,
the holy Word of God. Govern my daily life with

your strong yet tender care. Show me the way to redemption. Come, O sacred Lord of ancient Israel. Stretch out your mighty hand to set me free. Come, Flower of Jesse's stem, before whom the nations worship. Let nothing keep you from coming to our aid.

Come, O Key of David, break through the prison walls of death and release me from whatever holds me captive. Come, O Radiant Dawn, splendor of eternal light, and shine on all those who dwell in darkness and the shadow of death. Come, O King of the nations, the only joy of every human heart.

Come and save this helpless creature you fashioned from the dust. Come, Emmanuel, desire of the nations, Savior of all people. To you I entrust my intentions: (mention your request here).

DECEMBER

December 8

THE IMMACULATE CONCEPTION OF THE BLESSED VIRGIN MARY

THIS MOMENTOUS DAY, when the Blessed Virgin Mary is conceived in the womb of her mother, Anne, without original sin, is the beginning of so many other miracles. God does this in order to prepare his highly favored daughter to become the perfect Mother of God. But even before Mary gives birth to Jesus, the Immaculate Conception changes our lives. As a result of the Fall in the Garden of Eden, says the *Catechism of the Catholic Church*, "Adam and Eve … become afraid of the God of whom they have conceived a distorted image" (CCC 399, cf. Gen 3:5-10). And we who are born with original sin inherit this distorted conception of God. Everything we do depends on how we conceive of things. So God gives us a literally "impeccable" means of conceiving of him. Mary the Immaculate Conception is the living conception of God's own perfection.

The way that God conceives of his goodness is not an idea; it is a person for us to embrace. Now whenever we are tempted, like Adam and Eve, to make ourselves gods, there is a Mother looking at us with a gaze of immaculate love. The way back to paradise, the way to be like God as God himself desires us to be, is through a relationship with the New Eve, the Immaculate Conception. Just as the attractiveness of the forbidden tree in Eden moved Eve to eat of its fruit, so the beauty of the Immaculate Conception moves us to beg God for his forgiveness, his friendship, and his grace. God wants us to know him, respond to him, and love him in a manner "far beyond [our] own natural capacity" (CCC 52). Such an expectation would remain "inconceivable" unless God himself made it possible — which he does in the Immaculate Conception.

Through our devout union with the Mother of God, we can offer to God the obedience that Adam and Eve rejected. For the Father seeks to raise everyone to the holiness and perfection befitting the adopted children of God. Mary's unique excellence in the world of grace remains the divine method for making that happen.

NOVENA PRAYER

Blessed Virgin Mary, you are immaculately conceived. Your unique perfection is the fruit of the Father's goodness. It reveals the sanctity to which everyone is called. What Adam and Eve lost in Eden we have regained in the gift of your Immaculate

Conception, for you are destined to be the Mother of God and our Mother. The beauty of the Immaculate Conception moves us to beg God for his forgiveness, his friendship, and his grace.

May your Immaculate Conception save me from all worldly deception. O Immaculate Conception, break through the darkness of my life, even as God broke through the stranglehold of sin when you were conceived. Help me to live in hope by depending on your maternal love as the way to recover the innocence of Eden and to reach my eternal destiny, Jesus your Son. Calling upon your intercession, I offer you my intentions: (mention your request here).

December 12

OUR LADY OF GUADALUPE

BLESSED JOHN PAUL II, in the apostolic exhortation on the Church in America, reminds us that the Blessed Virgin

> is linked in a special way to … the peoples of America; through Mary they came to encounter the Lord…. Mary, by her motherly and merciful figure, was a great sign of the closeness of the Father and of Jesus

Christ, with whom she invites us to enter into communion.[1]

This feast commemorates the glorious apparitions in 1531 of Our Lady of Guadalupe to St. Juan Diego in Tepeyac, Mexico. Our Lady chooses to appear on the summit of a small hill where formerly had stood a temple to a pagan goddess whose hair was a mass of writhing snakes. That is, Mary chooses to insert herself with all her maternal love right into the heart of our idolatry. The Mother of God comes to the place where we are most distracted or distanced from God, to invite us back to his love. There she shows herself to be brimming with power.

In the miraculous image from that apparition, Our Lady stands with her foot on a crescent moon — a sign of her authority over one of the Aztec deities. Similarly, Mary's stance in front of the sun proclaims her supremacy over the dreaded Aztec sun god. And the green-blue hue of Mary's mantle proclaims her to be royalty. The very presence of Our Lady of Guadalupe moves us to surrender to God's mercy. But the Guadalupana also speaks. Her words are filled with tenderness and hope: "I am … the Mother of the True God. I will offer … all my love, my compassion, my help and my protection.… Do not be troubled or weighed down with grief. Am I not here who am your Mother?"[2]

And most awesome of all, she leaves us her image miraculously imprinted on the *tilma* of Juan Diego. After twenty years, the frail plant fibers of the cloak should have disintegrated. Yet after five hundred years, the heaven-made image is as vibrant and radiant as ever. We pray to remain as faithful to the Mother of God as she is persistent in remaining wondrously in our midst.

NOVENA PRAYER

Our Lady of Guadalupe, you are the perfect and ever Virgin Mary, Mother of the true God. You offer all people your love, your compassion, your help, and your protection. You show yourself the merciful Mother of all who love you and have confidence in you. Count me among your devout children. Hear my weeping and my sorrows, my necessities and my misfortunes. Save me from being troubled or weighed down with worry. Under your shadow and protection, keep me from fear, and prevent me from being grieved or disturbed by anything.

May I look at you and listen to you, and allow the mystery of your wondrous apparition to penetrate my heart, which I offer to you. Just as your miraculous image has remained for over five hun-

dred years, stay at the center of my faith. Confident
in your powerful intercession, I offer you my inten-
tions: (mention your request here).

December 25

THE NATIVITY OF THE LORD
(CHRISTMAS)

"LOWER YOUR HEAVENS AND COME DOWN" (Ps
143:5, The Grail). The psalmist's plea expresses the
urgent longing of every human heart. We want
to meet the One who loved us into existence. We
want the ability to listen to his voice and gaze upon
his face, like one friend to another. We want God
to become our companion, for to be human is
to *be in expectation* of this Someone who comes
to reveal us to ourselves. "God's Son came in the
flesh," says St. Bernard, "so that mortal human beings could see and recognize God's kindness."[3]

The method God employs to lead his people
into the mystery of the Incarnate Christ proceeds
"from the visible to the invisible" (CCC 1075).
"Knowledge of God is possible only through the
gift of God's love becoming visible" (Pope Benedict XVI).[4] Thus we pray in Preface I of the Nativity of the Lord: "In the mystery of the Word made

flesh a new light of your glory has shone upon the eyes of our mind, so that, as we recognize in him God made visible, we may be caught up through him in love of things invisible."

"The Word becomes flesh … *in order to save us by reconciling us with God*," to give us an infallible and concrete way of knowing God's love, "*to be our model of holiness*," and to make us " '*partakers of the divine nature*' (2 Pet 1:4)" (CCC 457, 459, and 460). The total impulse of Christ's new life is Eucharistic: from the moment of his birth, Jesus acts to give us his very self. For " 'by his Incarnation, he, the Son of God, has in a certain way united himself' (*GS* 22 § 2)" with every human being (CCC 521). The life he lives is not for him but for us; Jesus enables us to live in him the human life he lives, and he lives it in us and with us (see CCC 519).

"Behold, the Lamb of God" (Jn 1:29) — that is, behold the Lamb born to be sacrificed for our sins. O come, let us adore our Incarnate Savior who comes as a baby lest we be terrified — who comes in the aspect of one who does not judge.

NOVENA PRAYER

Incarnate Savior, you were born in darkness: come into my darkness, my doubts, and whatever makes me despondent and depressed. You were turned away by the innkeeper: turn me out of my resistance to God and whatever keeps me closed in on myself. You came in the piercing cold: come into my soul made cold by my sins. You were born in a stable: come into everything in my life that is unstable.

You came cared for by Joseph: come into my fears, my hurts, my regrets, my disappointments, and whatever makes life seem meaningless. You came born of Mary: come into my loneliness with the love with which Mary loves you. You came to the heralding of angels: come into my cynicism, and let me adore your mystery. You came as an infant, lest I be terrified. Full of trust, I offer you my intentions: (mention your request here).

December 28

THE HOLY INNOCENTS, MARTYRS

AMONG THE IMMENSE THRONG gathered for the Sermon on the Mount, perhaps there was a mother, now in her fifties. She listened. And it was when she heard Jesus pronounce, "Blessed are those who are persecuted for righteousness' sake, for theirs is the kingdom of heaven" (Mt

5:10), that she began to weep. Because now, at last, after all these years, with these words, she could finally understand. She could begin to fathom why it happened that nightmarish night, some thirty years ago in Bethlehem, when the soldiers swept through the streets, slaying all of the baby boys. Her own newborn had been murdered. But now, in the face of this man (who reminded her of what her own grown son might have looked like had he lived), she knew there was a reason. With joy she thought, "Those who suffer what my little boy suffered are called 'blessed' … are promised the kingdom of God. Their massacre was not meaningless. Their lives were sacrificed for righteousness' sake."

And what is "righteousness"? Pope Benedict XVI says that "the 'I' of Jesus himself, fidelity to his person, becomes the criterion of righteousness…. He himself is the reference point of the righteous life, its goal and center."[5] We enter into this feast begging for the grace to live perfect fidelity to the person of Jesus Christ, for the day will come when we, too, will be persecuted for Christ. Maybe our persecution will not be as severe and brutal as the slaughter of the Holy Innocents; yet, all the same, only their childlike innocence will dispose us to face the envy and hostility to come.

The Church reminds us,

> In our own times, children suffer innumerable forms of violence which threaten their lives, dignity and right to education. On this day, it is appropriate to recall the vast host of children not yet born who have been killed under the cover of laws permitting abortion, which is an abominable crime.[6]

There is a hint of the Eucharist in the way the Byzantine Liturgy hails the martyrdom of the Innocents: "Herod became exceedingly angry, and had the infants harvested like lamenting wheat."[7]

NOVENA PRAYER

Most merciful Father, as we prepare for the feast of the Holy Innocents, we call to mind all those who are hated and persecuted because of their witness to your Son. We pray in a special way for unborn children, for children who suffer from abuse, for orphans, for refugees, and for all children deprived of the respect and love that is their right as human beings.

Your Son teaches us that to be made worthy of heaven we must change and become like little chil-

dren. Convert us and help us to become like these little children who so closely resembled Christ that they were martyred for bearing his image. Help me live out my faith in heroic defense of all human life. May I help to slay the culture of death. United with the intercession of the Holy Innocents, I offer you my intentions: (make your request here).

December 30

THE HOLY FAMILY OF JESUS, MARY, AND JOSEPH

WHAT THE FEAST of the Holy Family proclaims to the world is that God himself belongs to a human family, and we are destined to be part of it. The *Catechism of the Catholic Church* points out that "Christ chose to be born and to grow up in the [embrace] of the holy family of Joseph and Mary" — a communion that is a foreshadowing of the Church itself — for "the Church is nothing other than 'the family of God' " (CCC 1655). The mystery of the Holy Family reveals that what now dominates the world, thanks to the Incarnation, is belonging, companionship, and community. The curse of loneliness, which lies at the root of human misery and wretchedness, has met its end.

We know how much we count on our own family to help us mature and become the persons we are meant to be. Simone Weil once said that "there is not a single thing in me that does not have its origin in the meeting between my father and my mother."[8] The family is that indispensable place where we first find ourselves, we try out our personality, we take risks, we receive our identity, we learn to love, and we realize that happiness is about self-sacrifice. Nowhere like in the family can our greatest needs be expressed. At home we can be at our worst and yet still be accepted, encouraged, counseled, corrected, forgiven, provided for, and loved.

All the same, we know too well that not every family is "holy." And so we look to the Holy Family to fill up what is lacking in our own — to "adopt us" spiritually. The Holy Family is holy because God in Jesus Christ is the center of it. We ask to share in the faith, hope, and love of the Holy Family so as to enter into the life of the Blessed Trinity, which the Holy Family images. The proof of the holiness of our family is our willingness to be witnesses. "The family has the mission to guard, reveal and communicate love," says Blessed John Paul II, "and this is a living reflection of and a real sharing in God's love for humanity."[9]

NOVENA PRAYER

Lord Jesus, what makes the Holy Family holy is your presence in the marital life of Mary and Joseph. Let me share in the love and grace of the Holy Family. Help me to live my own family life with sentiments of greater charity, gratitude, self-sacrifice, and trust. Make me selfless and generous in assisting the members of my family, especially in times of hardship. May all the graces that infused the life of the Holy Family permeate my own. Heal the divisions in my family. Bring reconciliation.

The Christian family is a reflection of the loving covenant uniting Christ with the Church. Make my family zealous in witnessing to the faith and in serving the needs of other families. Help me to love other people as my own brothers and sisters. Only Son of God, you who are my brother, receive the intentions I offer you: (mention your request here).

December 31

NEW YEAR'S EVE

TO PREPARE DEVOUTLY for the coming of a new year is to keep vigil — something expressly Christian. Repeatedly in the Gospels, Jesus commands his followers to "Keep watch" (for example, Mt

24:42-43 and Mk 13:35, 37). What consoles Jesus Christ the night before he dies is the presence of disciples in Gethsemane who will remain with him and watch (see Mk 14:34). Our vigilant attention to events yet to happen remains a distinguishing mark of Christians: we have a future. As Pope Benedict XVI explains, it is not that we know the details of what awaits us, but that we know that our "life will not end in emptiness."[10] This changes our whole perception of time, for we live in hope.

When the fullness of time had come, God sent his Son as Redeemer and Savior to be the fulfillment of all time, the center of all history. We reverence that miracle by spending the time God has allotted us as well as we possibly can. This means not being anxious, since none of us can add even a second to our span of life (see Mt 6:27, 34). Rather, we live abandoned to the sacrament of the present moment, for "with the Lord one day is as a thousand years" (2 Pt 3:8). The heart of our prayer is the trustful petition, "Give us this day our daily bread."

At the same time, we attend to the coming of "the day of Jesus Christ" (Phil 1:6). The Lord warns: "Take heed, watch and pray; for you do not know when the time will come" (Mk 13:33). As St. Peter puts it: "The day of the Lord will come like a thief.... What sort of persons ought you to be in lives of holiness and godliness, waiting for

and hastening the coming of the day of God....
We wait for new heavens and a new earth in which
righteousness dwells (see 2 Pt 3:10, 11-12, 13)

"So then, as we have opportunity, let us do
good to all men" (Gal 6:10), rejoicing that "every
beginning has a magic about it that protects us
and helps us live" (Herman Hesse).[11]

NOVENA PRAYER

*Loving Father, the communion of hope we live
with you reassures us that we have a future. We
live with the certainty of faith that our life will
not end in emptiness. Help me live with reverence
each moment of my life, acknowledging time as a
gift of mercy from you. For with you, one day is
as a thousand years. May I always use my time
constructively, in a manner beneficial to my sanctification. Save me from procrastination, from
idleness, and from wasting time. Protect me from
anxiety and worry.*

*Thank you for the past year and all the many
blessings you have bestowed upon me. As we await
the New Year, I thank you for this new beginning.
Keep me watchful for the day of the Lord. United
with your beloved Son, who entered time to save us
from our sins, I offer my intentions: (mention your
request here).*

ACKNOWLEDGMENTS

APPENDIX

(Note: The following feasts and observances are listed in chronological order.)

Feasts of the Lord

Feasts of the Blessed Virgin Mary

Other Liturgical Feasts

Other Observances

NOTES

Foreword

1. *Directory on Popular Piety and the Liturgy*, 32, www.vatican.va.
2. St. Augustine, from a letter to Proba, *The Liturgy of the Hours*, Vol. IV, Office of Readings, Twenty-Ninth Sunday in Ordinary Time.
3. St. Jerome, *Against Jovinianus*, Book I.16.
4. The source for the information in this and the following paragraph is Kurt Lampe, "A Twelfth-Century Text on the Number Nine and Divine Creation: A New Interpretation of Boethian Cosmology?" *Mediaeval Studies* 67 (2005): 1-26.

January

1. Alice Miller, *The Drama of the Gifted Child: The Search for the True Self* (New York: Basic Books, 1997), p. 27.
2. Blessed John Paul II, *Gift and Mystery* (New York: Doubleday, 1996), pp. 28-29.
3. Cited in *Christ Our Light: Patristic Readings on Gospel Themes, Vol. 1, Advent-Pentecost*, translated and edited by friends of Henry Ashworth (Riverdale, MD: Exordium, 1981), p. 64.
4. *Directory on Popular Piety and the Liturgy*, 117.
5. Servais Pinckaers, O.P., *The Pursuit of Happiness — God's Way* (New York: Alba House, 1988), pp. 154, 160.
6. St. Peter Chrysologus, http://catholicradiodramas.com/saints/p-s/peter-chrysologus/blessed-are-the-peacemakers/.

7. Joseph Ratzinger, *Seeking God's Face* (Chicago: Franciscan Herald Press, 1982), pp. 32-34.

8. Pope Benedict XVI, Message for World Day of Peace 2012 (January 1, 2012), 5.

9. Joseph Ratzinger, *Behold The Pierced One* (San Francisco: Ignatius, 1982), pp. 108-109.

10. Rama Coomaraswamy, *The Invocation of the Name of Jesus: As Practiced in the Western Church* (Louisville, KY: Fons Vitae, 1999), pp. 77-78.

11. Richard Rolle, *The Form of Perfect Living and Other Prose Treatises*, Geraldine E. Hodgson, trans. (London: Thomas Baker, 1910), pp. 53-54.

12. Pope Benedict XVI, World Youth Day, Meeting with Seminarians, Cologne (August 19, 2005), www.vatican.va.

13. *The Collected Works of Edith Stein: The Hidden Life*, Waltraut Stein, Ph.D., trans. (Washington, DC: ICS, 1992), pp. 110-112.

14. Fyodor Dostoevsky, *The Possessed*.

15. St. Leo the Great, *Sermo 6 in Nativitate Domini*, 2-3, 5: *PL* 54, 213-216.

16. Charles Dickens, *A Christmas Carol*, Stave I, www.gutenberg.com.

17. *Directory on Popular Piety and the Liturgy*, 182.

18. *The Roman Missal*, third edition, Friday of Holy Week, The Passion of the Lord; Mass for the Unity of Christians, Collect A and Collect B.

19. Pope Benedict XVI, *Jesus of Nazareth*, Vol. 2 (San Francisco: Ignatius, 2011), p. 96.

20. Pope Benedict XVI, *Caritas in Veritate* (2009), 28, www.vatican.va.

21. Blessed John Paul II, *Evangelium Vitae* (1995), 80-81, www.vatican.va.

22. Joseph Ratzinger, *The Nature and Mission of Theology* (San Francisco: Ignatius, 1995), p. 58.

23. Blessed John Paul II, *Prayers and Devotions: 365 Daily Meditations*, Bishop Peter Van Lierde, ed. (New York: Penguin, 1984), Ash Wednesday.

24. Message of Benedict XVI for Lent 2010 (October 30, 2009), www.vatican.va.

February

1. *Gaudium et Spes*, 24, www.vatican.va.

2. Message of the Holy Father Pope John Paul II for the First Annual World Day of the Sick (October 21, 1992), 1, www.vatican.va; emphasis in original.

3. Pope Benedict XVI, *Spe Salvi* (2007), 37, www.vatican.va.

4. Léon Bloy, http://thinkexist.com/quotation/there-are-places-in-the-heart-that-do-not-yet/348382.html.

5. Paul Claudel, epistle.us/inspiration/hispresence.html.

6. Blessed John Paul II, *Salvifici Doloris* (1984), 26, 27, www.vatican.va; emphasis in original.

7. Pope Leo XIII, Brief of September 8, 1901: 21 *Acta Leonis* XIII, 159-160.

8. *Directory on Popular Piety and the Liturgy*, 125.

9. Cited in Hans Urs von Balthasar, *The Grain of Wheat* (San Francisco: Ignatius, 1995), p. 45.

10. Pope Benedict XVI, *Verbum Domini* (2010), 26, www.vatican.va.

11. Raniero Cantalamessa, O.F.M. Cap., *Life in Christ* (Collegeville: Liturgical Press, 2002), p. 119.

12. Hans Urs von Balthasar, *Two Sisters in the Spirit* (San Francisco: Ignatius, 1998), p. 250.

13. Pope Benedict XVI, *Holiness Is Always in Season* (San Francisco: Ignatius, 2011), p. 67.
14. Colman O'Neil, *Sacramental Realism* (New York: Scepter, 1998), p. 30.

March

1. Blessed John Paul II, *Guardian of the Redeemer* (1989), 20, www.vatican.va.
2. Ibid., 19.
3. Ibid., 20; emphasis mine.
4. Jacques-Bénigne Bossuet, *Devotion to the Blessed Virgin* (London: Longmans, Green, 1899), p. 69.
5. Cesare Pavese, http://www.traces-cl.com/2006E/10/ladyourbeauty.html.
6. Blessed John Paul II, *Redemptoris Mater* (1987), 28, www.vatican.va.
7. Cited in Bossuet, *Devotion to the Blessed Virgin*, p. 3.
8. St. John of the Cross, *The Ascent of Mount Carmel*, Kieran Kavanaugh, O.C.D., and Otilio Rodriguez, O.C.D., trans. (Washington, DC: Institute of Carmelite Studies, 1979), pp. 124-125.
9. Hans Urs von Balthasar, *Heart of the World* (San Francisco: Ignatius, 1980), pp. 27-28, 183.
10. St. John of the Cross, *The Ascent of Mount Carmel*, pp. 124-125.
11. *The Liturgy of the Hours*, Vol. III, Ant. 3 for Daytime Prayer, Saturday of Week III, copyright © 1970, 1973, 1975, International Committee on English in the Liturgy (ICEL). All rights reserved.
12. Blessed John Paul II, *Pastores Dabo Vobis* (1992), 12, 15, www.vatican.va.

13. Ibid., 72, 78, 82.

14. Catherine de Hueck Doherty, *Dear Father: A Message of Love to Priests* (Combermere, Ontario, Canada: Madonna House, 1988), p. 66

15. Joseph Ratzinger, *Introduction to Christianity* (San Francisco: Ignatius, 1990), p. 215.

16. St. Hilary (Lib. 8, 13-16: PL 10, 246-249), *Liturgy of the Hours*, Office of Readings, Wednesday of the Fourth Week of Easter.

17. Cited in Massimo Camisasca, *Together on the Road: A Vision of Lived Communion for the Church and the Priesthood* (Boston: Pauline, 2005), p. 36.

18. Blessed John Paul II, *Crossing the Threshold of Hope* (New York: Knopf, 1995), p. 66.

19. Joseph Ratzinger, *The God of Jesus Christ: Meditations on the Triune God* (San Francisco: Ignatius, 2008), p. 55; *Salt of the Earth: The Church at the End of the Millennium* (San Francisco: Ignatius, 1997), p. 27.

20. Pope Benedict XVI, *Spe Salvi*, 2.

21. Ibid., 3.

22. Ibid., 11, 12.

23. St. Thomas Aquinas, *Summa Theologica*, II-II.20.3.

24. Julián Carrón, *Friends, That Is, Witnesses*, Patrick Stevenson, trans. (Milan, Italy: Traces Booklets, 2007), p. 19.

April

1. Cited in Luigi Giussani, *You Live for Love of Something Happening Now* (Rimini, Italy: Fraternity of Communion and Liberation, 2006), p. 28.

2. *Avvenire* (April 15, 2006), www.avvenire.it.

3. Luigi Giussani, *Why the Church*?, V. Hewitt, trans. (Montreal: McGill-Queens, 2001), pp. 94-95.

4. Pope Benedict XVI, *Jesus of Nazareth*, Vol. 2, p. 275.

5. Joseph Ratzinger, *Introduction to Christianity*, pp. 229-230.

6. Mother Marie des Douleurs, *Joy Out of Sorrow* (Newman Press, 1958), pp.146-148.

7. Blessed John Paul II, Homily, Divine Mercy Sunday (April 22, 2001), www.vatican.va.

8. *Directory on Popular Piety and the Liturgy*, 154.

9. Josef Pieper, *The Concept of Sin* (South Bend, IN: St. Augustine's, 2001), pp. 80-81.

10. St. Thomas Aquinas, *Summa Theologica*, I.21.4, *ad* 4.

11. Blessed John Paul II, *Memory and Identity: Conversations at the Dawn of a Millennium* (New York: Rizzoli, 2005), pp. 6-7.

12. Blessed John Paul II, *Pastores Dabo Vobis*, 19.

13. Ibid., 2.

14. Ibid., 34.

15. Karol Wojtyla (Blessed John Paul II), *Sign of Contradiction* (New York: Seabury, 1979), p. 130.

16. Blessed John Paul II, *Vita Consecrata* (1996), 16, www.vatican.va; emphasis in original.

May

1. Blessed John Paul II, *Laborem Exercens* (1981), 25, quoting *Gaudium et Spes*, 34, www.vatican.va; emphasis in original.

2. Louis Lavelle, *The Dilemma of Narcissus* (Burdett, NY: Larson, 1993), pp. 79-80.

3. M. D. Philippe, *The Worship of God*, Dom Mark Pontifex, trans. (New York: Hawthorn, 1963), pp. 123-124.

4. Lorenzo Albacete, *God at the Ritz. Attraction to Infinity* (New York: Crossroad, 2007), p. 141.

5. Luigi Giussani, *Why the Church?*, p. 218.

6. Blessed John Paul II, *Rosarium Virginis Mariae* (2002), 11, www.vatican.va; emphasis in original.

7. Bossuet, *Devotion to the Blessed Virgin*, p. 84.

8. St. Louis de Montfort, *True Devotion*, Part I, Ch. 2, Art. 4, Malachy G. Carroll, trans. (Langley Bucks, England: St. Paul, 1962).

9. *The Works of St. Augustine: Sermons 111/7*, Edmund Hill, O.P., trans. (New Rochelle, NY: New City Press, 1993), p. 229 (Sermon 264.4).

10. St. Leo the Great (Sermo 2 de Ascensione 1-4: PL 54, 397-399), *The Liturgy of the Hours*, Vol. II, Office of Readings, Friday of the Sixth Week of Easter.

11. Pope Benedict XVI, *Jesus of Nazareth*, Vol. 2, pp. 281, 284.

12. Pope Benedict XVI, *Dogma and Preaching* (San Francisco: Ignatius, 2011), pp. 62-63.

June

1. St. Thomas Aquinas, *In 2 Corinthians*, ch. 3, lect. 3.

2. Cited in M. F. Toal, ed., *The Sunday Sermons of the Great Fathers*, Vol. Three (San Francisco: Ignatius, 2000), p. 44.

3. Ibid., p. 51.

4. Ibid., p. 8.

5. Ibid., p. 18.

6. St. Cyril of Alexandria (Lib. 10: PG 74, 434), *The Liturgy of the Hours*, Vol. II, Office of Readings, Thursday of the Seventh Week of Easter.

7. St. Thomas Aquinas, *Summa Theologica*, I.31.3, *ad* 1.

8. *The Roman Missal*, third edition, Prayer at the Cleansing of the Vessels.

9. Ibid.

10. *Directory on Popular Piety and the Liturgy*, 166.

11. *The Spiritual Direction of Saint Claude de la Colombière*, Mother M. Philip, trans. (San Francisco: Ignatius, 1998), pp. 23, 24.

12. Msgr. Robert Hugh Benson, *The Friendship of Christ* (Westminster, MD: Newman Press, 1955), pp. 6-7.

13. *Thoughts and Sayings of Saint Margaret Mary for Every Day of the Year*, Srs. of the Visitation, trans. (Rockford, IL: TAN, 1986), #29.

14. Pope Benedict XVI, Homily, Solemnity of the Sacred Heart of Jesus (June 19, 2009), www.vatican.va.

15. *Directory on Popular Piety and the Liturgy*, 174.

16. St. John Eudes, *The Admirable Heart of Mary*, Charles di Targiani and Ruth Hauser, trans. (New York: P. J. Kenedy, 1948), p. 246.

17. St. Louis de Montfort, *True Devotion*, Part II, Ch. 3, Art. 2.

18. *The Works of Saint Augustine*, III/10, p. 372.

July

1. St. Clement of Rome, First Epistle to the Corinthians, 7:4. http://www.ccel.org/ccel/schaff/anf01.ii.ii.vii.html.

2. St. John Chrysostom, *Homilies on St. John*, 1-47,
    Sr. Thomas Aquinas Goggin, S.C.H., trans.
    (Washington, DC: Catholic University of America
    Press, 1967), p. 469.

3. St. Gregory the Great (Lib. 13, 21-23: PL 75, 1028-
    1029), *The Liturgy of the Hours*, Office of Readings,
    Friday of the Third Week of Lent.

4. Raniero Cantalamesa, O.F.M. Cap., *The Eucharist,
    Our Sanctification*, Frances L. Vialla, trans.
    (Collegeville, MN: Liturgical Press, 1993), p. 40.

5. St. Catherine of Siena, *The Dialogue*, #66, Suzanne
    Noffke, O.P., trans. (New York: Paulist, 1980).

6. *The Letters of Catherine of Siena*, Vol. II, Suzanne
    Noffke, ed. (MRTS, 2001), Letter T210/G138, p. 236.

7. St. Robert Southwell, http://hieronymopolis
    .wordpress.com/2010/08/13/certaine-iaculatorie-
    praiers-written-by-the-rev-fa-r-s-1600/.

8. St. John Chrysostom, op. cit.

9. Blessed John Paul II, *Crossing the Threshold of Hope*,
    pp. 120-121.

10. Pope Benedict XVI, Message for the Twenty-Sixth
    World Youth Day, 2011 (August 6, 2010), www
    .vatican.va.

11. Blessed John Paul II, *Vita Consecrata*, 70, www
    .vatican.va.

12. Cited in Hans Urs von Balthasar, *The Grain of
    Wheat*, p. 37.

August

1. Massimo Camisasca, *The Challenge of Fatherhood*,
    Adrian Walker, trans. (New York: Human
    Adventure Books, 2009), p. 55.

2. Luigi Giussani, *At the Origin of the Christian Claim* (Montreal: McGill-Queens University Press, 1998), p. 104.

3. St. Leo the Great (Sermo 51, 3-4, 8: PL 54, 310-311. 313J), *The Liturgy of the Hours*, Office of Readings, Second Sunday of Lent.

4. St. Thomas Aquinas, *Summa Theologica*, III. 45. 1.

5. Luigi Giussani, *At the Origin of the Christian Claim*, p. 102; *The Psalms*, William Vouk, tr. (New York: Crossroad, 2004), p. 151; *Why the Church?*, pp. 180, 182.

6. Joseph Raya and Jose De Vinck, *Byzantine Daily Worship* (Allendale, NJ: Alleluia, 1989), p. 748.

7. St. Thomas Aquinas, *Commentary on the Hail Mary*.

8. Cited in David Supple, ed., *Virgin Wholly Marvelous* (Still River, MA: Ravengate, 1981), p. 107.

9. St. Amadeus of Lausanne, *Eight Homilies on the Praises of Blessed Mary*, Grace Perigo, trans. (Collegeville, MN: Cistercian, 2006), p. 14.

10. Blessed John Paul II, *Theotokos: Woman, Mother, Disciple* (Boston: Pauline, 1999), p. 38.

11. Cited in Luigi Gambero, *Mary in the Middle Ages* (San Francisco: Ignatius, 2005), p. 200.

12. Blessed John Paul II, *Theotokos*, p. 212.

13. Cited in St. Louis de Montfort, *True Devotion*, Part II, Ch. 1, Art. 3.

14. St. Louis de Montfort, *True Devotion*, Introduction.

15. St. Thomas Aquinas, http://www.catholictradition .org/Mary/mary18a.htm.

16. Blessed Henry Suso, http://archive.org/stream/ maryspraise00chanuoft/maryspraise00chanuoft_ djvu.txt.

September

1. Cited in John Saward, *The Beauty of Holiness and the Holiness of Beauty* (San Francisco: Ignatius, 1997), p. 35.
2. For example, see St. Gregory Palamas, *The Saving Work of Christ*, Christopher Veniamin, ed. (Waymart, PA: Mount Thabor, 2008), pp. 4, 2.
3. Blessed John Paul II, *Theotokos*, p. 36.
4. Johannes Tauler, *Spiritual Conferences* (Rockford, IL: Tan, 1979), p. 168.
5. Bossuet, *Devotion to the Blessed Virgin*, pp. 40-41.
6. Raya and De Vinck, *Byzantine Daily Worship*, p. 439.
7. St. Gregory Palamas, http://www.stsymeon.com/palamas_quotes.html.
8. Cited in Supple, *Virgin Wholly Marvelous*, p. 9.
9. Ibid., p. 8.
10. St. Louis de Montfort, *True Devotion*, Part II, Ch. 3. Art. 1.
11. Ibid., Part II, Ch. 1, Art. 3.
12. http://catholicforum.fisheaters.com/index.php?topic=3443702.0.
13. Cited in Gambero, *Mary in the Middle Ages*, p. 140.
14. www.johnsanidopoulos.com/2011/05/st-john-chrysostoms-homily-on-cemetery.html.
15. Paul Claudel, *The Satin Slipper*, Father John O'Connor, trans. (New York: Sheed and Ward, 1945), p.197.
16. Simon Tugwell, *The Beatitudes* (Springfield, IL: Templegate, 1986), p. 135.
17. Camisasca, *Together on the Road*, p. 39.
18. Blessed John Paul II, *Theotokos*, pp. 27, 184.

19. Cited in Supple, *Virgin Wholly Marvelous*, p. 73.
20. Ibid., p. 116.
21. Blessed John Paul II, *Salvifici Doloris*, 26.
22. *Wisdom's Watch Upon the Hours, The Fathers of the Church*, Volume 4, Edmund Colledge, O.S.A., trans. (Washington, DC: Catholic University of America, 1994), p. 222.
23. Blessed John Paul II, *Salvifici Doloris*, 30.
24. *The Faith of the Early Fathers*, Volume I, p. 387.
25. Adrienne von Speyr, *The Gates of Eternal Life* (San Francisco: Ignatius, 1983), p. 105.
26. Jacobus de Voragine, *The Golden Legend: Readings on the Saints*, Volume II, William Granger Ryan, trans. (Princeton, NJ: Princeton University Press, 1993), pp. 208-210.
27. http://www.earlychristianwritings.com/text/shepherd.html.

October

1. *Commentary on Matthew*, quoted in "Guardian Angel," the Catholic Encyclopedia (New York: The Encyclopedia Press, 1912), vol. 7, p. 49.
2. St. Thomas Aquinas, *Summa Theologica*, I.113.1, 4, 5, 6.
3. Cited in Cardinal Jean Daniélou, *The Angels and Their Mission* (Allen, TX: Thomas More, 1987), pp. 75-76.
4. Ibid.
5. Simon Tugwell, O.P., *Prayer in Practice* (Springfield, IL: Templegate, 1974), pp. 105-106.
6. *The Hidden Life: The Collected Works of Edith Stein*, Volume Five, p. 279.

7. Blessed John Paul II, *Redemptoris Missio* (1990), 1, 2, www.vatican.va.
8. Camisasca, *Together on the Road*, p. 64.
9. http://cl-event.blogspot.com/2008_07_06_archive.html.
10. *Fraternity and Mission*, Vol. IX, n. 1, February-March 2005, p. 1.

November

1. Pope Benedict XVI, Homily, World Mission Sunday (October 23, 2005), www.vatican.va.
2. http://penitents.org/repair10.htm.
3. St. Thomas Aquinas, *Summa Theologica*, Supplement, Q. 72.
4. Joseph Cardinal Ratzinger (Pope Benedict XVI), *God and the World: A Conversation with Peter Sewald* (San Francisco: Ignatius, 2002), pp. 129-130.
5. *The Spiritual Direction of Saint Claude de la Colombière*, p. 137.
6. *Treatise on Purgatory*, ch. 8, http://www.ewtn.com/library/spirit/catpur.txt.
7. Ibid., XVI, IX.
8. Blessed John Paul II, *Rosarium Virginis Mariae*, 20.
9. Raya and De Vinck, *Byzantine Daily Worship*, p. 517.
10. *Mary the Mother of God: Sermons by Saint Gregory Palamas*, Christopher Veniamin, ed. (South Canaan, PA: Mount Thabor, 2005), p. 33.

December

1. Blessed John Paul II, *Ecclesia in America* (1999), 11, www.vatican.va.
2. http://www.ourladyofguadalupe.info/.
3. http://www.angelfire.com/ga4/j_timberlake0/B446. htm.
4. Pope Benedict XVI, *Jesus of Nazareth*, Vol. 1 (San Francisco: Ignatius, 2008), p. 194.
5. Pope Benedict XVI, *Jesus of Nazareth*, Vol. 1, p. 90.
6. *Directory on Popular Piety and the Liturgy*, 113.
7. Raya and De Vinck, *Byzantine Daily Worship*, p. 576.
8. Cited in Raymond and Lauretta Seabeck, *The Smiling Pope: The Life and Teaching of John Paul I* (Huntington, IN: Our Sunday Visitor, 2004), p. 143.
9. Blessed John Paul II, *Familiaris Consortio* (1981), 17.
10. Pope Benedict XVI, *Spe Salvi*, 2.
11. http://mindmastery.wordpress.com/2007/02/17/ hermann-hesse-steps-stufen/